Current
CONTROVERSIES

W9-CIC-032

Homeschooling

Other Books in the Current Controversies Series

Homeschooling

Myra Immell, Book Editor

GREENHAVEN PRESS
A part of Gale, Cengage Learning

Detroit • New York • San Francisco • New Haven, Conn • Waterville, Maine • London

GALE
CENGAGE Learning

Christine Nasso, *Publisher*
Elizabeth Des Chenes, *Managing Editor*

For more information, contact:
Greenhaven Press
27500 Drake Rd.
Farmington Hills, MI 48331-3535
Or you can visit our Internet site at gale.cengage.com

For product information and technology assistance, contact us at

Gale Customer Support, 1-800-877-4253
For permission to use material from this text or product, submit all requests online at www.cengage.com/permissions

Further permissions questions can be emailed to permissionrequest@cengage.com

Articles in Greenhaven Press anthologies are often edited for length to meet page requirements. In addition, original titles of these works are changed to clearly present the main thesis and to explicitly indicate the author's opinion. Every effort is made to ensure that Greenhaven Press accurately reflects the original intent of the authors. Every effort has been made to trace the owners of copyrighted material.

Cover image © Elena Elisseeva, 2008. Used under license from Shutterstock.com.

LIBRARY OF CONGRESS CATALOGING-IN-PUBLICATION DATA

Homeschooling / Myra Immell, book editor.
    p. cm. -- (Current controversies)
    Includes bibliographical references and index.
    ISBN-13: 978-0-7377-4140-7 (hardcover)
    ISBN-13: 978-0-7377-4141-4 (pbk.)
    1. Home schooling. I. Immell, Myra.
    LC40.H6673 2009
    371.04'2--dc22

                                                    2008033984

Printed in the United States of America
1 2 3 4 5 6 7 12 11 10 09 08

Contents

Chapter 2: Is Homeschooling a Good Option?

Chapter 3: Should Homeschooling Be Regulated?

Chapter 4: Should Homeschooled Children Have Access to Public School Resources?

Foreword

By definition, controversies are "discussions of questions in which opposing opinions clash" (Webster's Twentieth Century Dictionary Unabridged). Few would deny that controversies are a pervasive part of the human condition and exist on virtually every level of human enterprise. Controversies transpire between individuals and among groups, within nations and between nations. Controversies supply the grist necessary for progress by providing challenges and challengers to the status quo. They also create atmospheres where strife and warfare can flourish. A world without controversies would be a peaceful world; but it also would be, by and large, static and prosaic.

The Series' Purpose

The purpose of the *Current Controversies* series is to explore many of the social, political, and economic controversies dominating the national and international scenes today. Titles selected for inclusion in the series are highly focused and specific. For example, from the larger category of criminal justice, *Current Controversies* deals with specific topics such as police brutality, gun control, white collar crime, and others. The debates in *Current Controversies* also are presented in a useful, timeless fashion. Articles and book excerpts included in each title are selected if they contribute valuable, long-range ideas to the overall debate. And wherever possible, current information is enhanced with historical documents and other relevant materials. Thus, while individual titles are current in focus, every effort is made to ensure that they will not become quickly outdated. Books in the *Current Controversies* series will remain important resources for librarians, teachers, and students for many years.

In addition to keeping the titles focused and specific, great care is taken in the editorial format of each book in the series. Book introductions and chapter prefaces are offered to provide background material for readers. Chapters are organized around several key questions that are answered with diverse opinions representing all points on the political spectrum. Materials in each chapter include opinions in which authors clearly disagree as well as alternative opinions in which authors may agree on a broader issue but disagree on the possible solutions. In this way, the content of each volume in *Current Controversies* mirrors the mosaic of opinions encountered in society. Readers will quickly realize that there are many viable answers to these complex issues. By questioning each author's conclusions, students and casual readers can begin to develop the critical thinking skills so important to evaluating opinionated material.

Current Controversies is also ideal for controlled research. Each anthology in the series is composed of primary sources taken from a wide gamut of informational categories including periodicals, newspapers, books, U.S. and foreign government documents, and the publications of private and public organizations. Readers will find factual support for reports, debates, and research papers covering all areas of important issues. In addition, an annotated table of contents, an index, a book and periodical bibliography, and a list of organizations to contact are included in each book to expedite further research.

Perhaps more than ever before in history, people are confronted with diverse and contradictory information. During the Persian Gulf War, for example, the public was not only treated to minute-to-minute coverage of the war, it was also inundated with critiques of the coverage and countless analyses of the factors motivating U.S. involvement. Being able to sort through the plethora of opinions accompanying today's major issues, and to draw one's own conclusions, can be a complicated and frustrating struggle. It is the editors' hope that *Current Controversies* will help readers with this struggle.

Introduction

"Unlike the diplomas received by most public—and private—school students, diplomas issued to homeschooled students are not always recognized by most states."

According to the National Center for Education Statistics, an estimated 1.1 million students in the United States are homeschooled. About 315,000 of these students are of high-school age. Like public school students, homeschoolers who have completed their high school course work graduate and receive some sort of diploma.

Unlike the diplomas received by most public—and private—school students, diplomas issued to homeschooled students are not always recognized by most states. Homeschoolers have a number of options for a diploma. Most, however, receive diplomas issued by their parents, who have homeschooled them in accordance with the graduation requirements they have set. To give the diploma more weight and, if necessary, provide proof that certain standards have been met, parents typically create and maintain a transcript that documents the student's academic record. Parent-issued diplomas are not accredited. They may be accepted by some employers and by some colleges and universities, but they are not recognized as valid in most states.

Even some state-issued diplomas for homeschooled students are not always recognized. Such was the case in Tennessee in 2008. Tennessee began recognizing homeschooling in 1985. The state offered several categories of diplomas, one of which is the category IV diploma issued to homeschooled students and church-related school students. These students did not need a public or accredited private school diploma to be hired for positions for which state law required a high school diploma. Their category IV diplomas were recognized in state institutions and for employment. A major controversy arose, however, in May 2008 when the Tennessee Department of Education declared it no longer would recognize Category IV diplomas. The basis for the decision was that the department had no way of telling what a homeschool diploma represented as it had no part in the selection of homeschool curriculum, teachers, or textbooks.

The ramifications of the department's decision were immediate and proved controversial. The category IV diplomas no longer were recognized by the Peace Officers Standards and Training Commission (POST), the Tennessee Police Training Organization, or the Department of Human Services, which sets policy for the hiring of day-care workers. These groups were required by statute to hire only individuals with recognized diplomas. Four day-care workers lost their jobs because their diplomas no longer were recognized. A police officer was told that if he wanted to keep his job he had to get his GED, commonly known as a General Equivalency Diploma. The officer had received his category IV diploma seven years earlier, had previously held various law-enforcement positions, had made perfect grades in graduating from a college law-enforcement certification class, and had an exemplary record. However, with his diploma no longer recognized, the POST declared he could not be certified as a police officer and could not hold his job. He was demoted to a desk job until he took and passed the GED—or until the Tennessee legislature passed a law making category IV diplomas acceptable for state-related kinds of employment.

Efforts put forth by Tennessee representative Mike Bell and others to have a bill passed that would make category IV diplomas valid and recognized by the state and its agencies proved unsuccessful. Critics of a bill proposed by Bell in 2008 argued that passage would give a legislative seal of approval to a homeschool or church-related school education when the state had no control over what was involved in that education. Others argued that passage would give special treatment to homeschool and church-related school students who were not required to take certain state-required proficiency exams, while public school students who had to take and subsequently failed the exams received a certificate of attendance instead of a regular diploma. Bell ultimately took his bill "off notice" and announced plans to bring a new bill to the House Education Committee in the near future.

The validity of homeschool diplomas is just one of a variety of homeschooling-related issues being debated nationwide today. The roots of homeschooling lie far back in history, long before universal public schooling was even a thought let alone a reality. The trend back to homeschooling that has become more prevalent in recent years continues to grow, and with it controversies surrounding even the most basic issues. In *Current Controversies: Homeschooling*, proponents of homeschooling and critics of homeschooling offer their differing viewpoints on several of those basic issues.

CHAPTER 1

Why Do Parents Choose to Homeschool?

Chapter Preface

If you ask parents who homeschool their children why they chose to do so you will get a variety of answers. The National Home Education Network (NHEN), an organization that advocates homeschooling, lists fifty-five reasons to homeschool. These range from "spend more time together as a family" to "children can learn to work for internal satisfaction rather than for external rewards" to "children's education can be more complete than what schools offer."

Some reasons, however, are more commonly voiced than others. Early on, for example, most parents homeschooled their children primarily for religious reasons. Later, in the mid-to-late 1990s, many parents still homeschooled primarily for religious reasons. But a good number also homeschooled to give their children a better education at home or because of what they considered "a poor learning environment at school."

Based on the National Center for Education Statistics (NCES) of the U.S. Department of Education Statistical Analysis Report "Homeschooling in the United States, 2003," issued in February 2006, those reasons still stand. Homeschooler parents who took part in the survey were given a set of reasons for homeschooling. First, the parents were asked which, if any of the reasons, applied to them. Concern about the environment of other schools, including safety, drugs, or negative peer pressure, was the reason for homeschooling cited most frequently as being applicable. Eighty-five percent of homeschooled students were being homeschooled, in part, because of that concern. The next two reasons most frequently cited were to provide religious or moral instruction (72 percent) and dissatisfaction with academic instruction at other schools (68 percent). A child's special needs was applicable for 28 percent of the parents; such other reasons as a child's choice, more control over what the child was learning, and flexibility were cited by 20 percent of the respondents; and a child's physical or mental health problem was named by 15 percent.

Next the parents were asked which one of the reasons was their most important for homeschooling. Thirty-one percent of homeschooled children had parents who cited concern about the environment of other schools, such as safety, drugs, or negative peer pressure, as the most important reason for homeschooling, and 30 percent had parents who said the most important reason was to provide religious or moral instruction. Another 16 percent of homeschooled students had parents who said dissatisfaction with the academic instruction available at other schools was their most important reason for homeschooling. Six percent cited a child's physical or mental health problem as the most important reason, and 7 percent cited a child's other special needs. Another 8 percent indicated other reasons, such as a child's choice, more control over what the child was learning, and flexibility, as most important.

One of the Frequently Asked Questions posted on the Web site of Homeschool Zone is "Why should I homeschool?" The response sums up the rationale for homeschooling of most homeschool parents and advocates: "I think the common denominator in many homeschoolers is that for whatever reason, homeschoolers feel that there is a better way for their children to learn or that the system has not addressed the needs of their children."

Homeschooling Helps Black Children Gain Educational Equality

Jennifer James

Jennifer James is the founding director of the National African-American Homeschoolers Alliance.

"Mommy, I finished my book. Do we still get to see the movie tomorrow?" my daughter Annlyel asked, triumphantly removing her bookmark from its place and closing her book.

"We sure do," I smiled. "You finished Harry Potter and, as promised, we're going to see the movie when it comes out tomorrow."

When my older daughter, then five, finished reading her first full-length novel—entirely on her own initiative—I knew at that moment that my husband, Michael, and I had made the right decision to homeschool our two children.

An Easy Decision

Opting to homeschool came quite easily for us, though we learned about it only by mere happenstance. Casually watching television one afternoon when Annlyel was still an infant, we watched as a homeschooled student competed quite well in the last rounds of the Scripps National Spelling Bee. We knew nothing about homeschooling, but just hearing the commentator speak the word homeschooled resonated deeply with us and instantly piqued our interest to the point of action.

The very next day, we set out on a fierce quest to learn as much about homeschooling as we could, and to gather the necessary information about how to begin homeschooling in

Jennifer James, "Homeschooling for Black Families," *Mothering*, January/February 2007, pp. 66–71. Reproduced by permission of the author.

our state, North Carolina. With the aid of a helpful local school administrator, we learned whom we needed to contact, then called our state's homeschooling organization.

"Surely we aren't the only black homeschoolers in America!" we often kidded aloud.

The rest is history. Before Annlyel could even sit up by herself, she had become a future homeschooled child. Just as quickly, we had become homeschooling parents. . . .

One reason Michael and I decided to homeschool was to ensure that our children received a sterling education. Based on what we learned about the steadily plummeting levels of achievement of large numbers of publicly schooled black children, we knew that that was not an option for our family. We also knew that private schools are extremely expensive. The prospect of homeschooling proved to be an excellent alternative for us—I was already a stay-at-home mother, and Michael and I are both excited about learning and are steadfastly focused on education. Homeschooling was perfect. We couldn't have been happier.

Unfulfilled promises prompt families such as ours to deem public education—in its present state—categorically unsuitable for black children.

Homeschooling Helps Achievement

What eventually dawned on us, however, was that we hadn't heard or read about, or run into, or known any black homeschoolers other than ourselves. "Surely we aren't the only black homeschoolers in America!" we often kidded aloud. But it felt that way. After noticing the absence of black homeschoolers in our area, and after a fruitless search of the Internet, I decided, in January 2003, to start the National African-

American Homeschoolers Alliance (NAAHA). Now four years old, NAAHA is the largest homeschooling organization for blacks in America, and provides the most comprehensive information and resources for black families on the Net. . . .

After speaking with hundreds of families across the country, I learned that blacks homeschool for the same reasons as other families, as well as for a unique set of reasons that do not apply to other races. For example, homeschooling is one way black children in America can gain true educational parity. Although many educational alternatives are becoming available, homeschooling parents are confident that they can educate their own children well enough that they will meet or exceed state and national standards and be ready for college. In so doing, these families reject the notion that their children cannot learn, or lack the capacity to learn. Most experts agree that in order for children to be well educated, parents must be actively involved in their education. This shift toward greater, if not primary, parental involvement will undoubtedly result in black children who achieve at levels that public schools cannot replicate, and who are subsequently better prepared for higher education. In fact, in one of the only studies to take a critical look at minority homeschoolers, Dr. Brian Ray of the National Home Education Research Institute found that minority and white homeschooled students both scored in the 87th percentile in reading; and in math, whites edged out minority homeschoolers by only five points—82nd and 77th percentiles, respectively.

One of the main sentiments echoed by black parents . . . is that they have to give their children a fighting chance in this world.

A Movement Away from Public Schooling

It is important to note that as the number of black homeschoolers increases, a noticeable divorce from public schooling—an educational option that blacks have, historically, been staunchly wedded to—is also taking place. In 2004, we all saw the celebrations, remembrances, symposiums, and conferences that marked the 50th anniversary of the Supreme Court's landmark *Brown v. Board of Education* ruling. Ever since this important decision, blacks have relied heavily, almost to a fault, on public education. After all, blacks fought hard to ensure that their children were afforded the same quality of education as everyone else. What they didn't count on was that the promises implied by *Brown v. Board of Education* would still be light-years away from fulfillment a half century later. Those unfulfilled promises prompt families such as ours to deem public education—in its present state—categorically unsuitable for black children.

If you look at the statistics of underachievement for black children, the ever-present achievement gap between black and white children, and the excessive dropout rates and generally unequal resources for black and inner-city schools, few can deny that public schools continue to fail the vast majority of black children. Even so, when black parents decide to homeschool, some educators consider this an act of disloyalty. Although some of that sentiment is beginning to wane, especially as reforms in the educational choices available to all parents become more widespread, there persists an overarching opinion that blacks, particularly those of us committed to education, should stay in and repair the public schools. While this may seem noble in many regards, black homeschoolers no longer want their children used as guinea pigs in educational experiments to see if their test scores will rise a percentage point or two. The expectation that black families should repair public education seems greater in black communities than in others. This is a distinct difference in how black homeschoolers are perceived, compared to others who opt for home education.

Another distinction: Blacks are homeschooling in growing numbers because they believe that is how they can better provide a high-quality, heritage-based education for their children. The many black homeschooling families I speak with across the country maintain that traditional education curricula neglect the full range of black history. The textbooks and curricula in traditional schools tend to focus on slavery, the Civil Rights Movement, and such obligatory historic figures as Harriet Tubman, Frederick Douglass, and Martin Luther King, Jr.—but little beyond that. Black families want their children to have a well-rounded education from a variety of standpoints and perspectives. Above all, they want their children to know that blacks have played important roles not only in US history, but in the history of the world. Parents believe that the time is ripe for their children to learn black and multicultural history on their own terms. Without a doubt, homeschooling lends itself to this end.

Not long ago, there was a general misconception that homeschooling was an option only for white middle- and upper-class families.

Education Is Vital

One of the main sentiments echoed by black parents from coast to coast, no matter where they live and no matter their socioeconomic status or family dynamic, is that they have to give their children a fighting chance in this world. They believe, as Michael and I do, that homeschooling is the best way to do that.

I often speak with parents who have three or four children, the older ones already having gone through the public education system but not achieving at levels acceptable to colleges. These parents are now determined to make a difference in the lives of their younger children. They often mention a subtle racism that begins in the early grades and say they wish they had taken control when those issues might still have been addressed and resolved. Parents cite instances where their children were inaccurately labeled "slow" and placed in remedial classes for the duration of their public school careers. They cite the absence of advanced-placement and honors courses in their children's schools, a lack of equal resources and technology, and constant finger-pointing among parents, teachers, and administrators, all of whom blame each other for the achievement gap. Although these parents attribute their children's lack of success to these variables, they are also quick to acknowledge the apathy about and lack of interest in education among some black students and their parents. By homeschooling, conscientious black families are countering these negative attitudes about learning and the peer-led disdain for education held by some blacks. They are, in effect, creating a movement of black families for whom education is vital to their children's success and the betterment of their communities. No longer accepting that their children must go to public school, they are instead standing up for home education, touting its advantages and praising its results.

I have spoken with many families who say that the potential rewards of homeschooling far outweigh any personal sacrifices they might have to make.

The Diversity of Black Homeschoolers

Not long ago, there was a general misconception that homeschooling was an option only for white middle- and upper-class families. Surprisingly, I regularly get calls and e-mails from black parents who are amazed that homeschooling is an option for them as well. Now that homeschooling stereotypes are being replaced by more accurate notions of who actually homeschools, increasing numbers of black families are joining the movement, setting up classrooms in their homes, and educating their children—to the tune of 103,000 black homeschooled children in the US.

As more blacks homeschool, it becomes increasingly apparent that black homeschooling families are as diverse as any other homeschooling group. Although there are no definitive statistics that reveal the specific demographics of black homeschoolers, I have learned through my work with the NAAHA that there are black single-parent homeschoolers, as well as homes in which the mother takes over the educational duties because she stays at home. There are black dual-income homeschooling families in which one parent homeschools during the day, the other during the evening. I have met several families in which grandparents homeschool their grandchildren. They may be retired, and teach their grandkids while the parents are at work, or they may be their grandkids' sole guardians and have the time and resources to teach them at home. There are sizable numbers of families such as our own, whose children are young and, barring unforeseen circumstances, will be homeschooled until they go to college. Other families are pulling their children out of school midstream in order to educate them themselves.

Some argue that homeschooling will never be an option for most blacks because of factors inherent in the black community, such as the large numbers of single-parent and dual-income homes. While statistics do not verify this, I have spoken with many families who say that the potential rewards of homeschooling far outweigh any personal sacrifices they might have to make. . . .

Black families practice a variety of homeschooling philosophies. Some are strict traditionalists because they want to ensure that their children will not fare worse educationally than they would in public schools. Others are more relaxed about their children's education, and are happy to let them learn from everyday living. These families believe that this will result not only in good learning, but in confident children who are excited about education. . . .

A Role for Support Groups

Local support groups are popping up all over the country. Like me, mothers and fathers are starting these groups because they want their children to see and socialize with other black homeschooled children. It is important that a child not feel isolated in a community in which he or she is the only black homeschooled student, or one of only a few. These parents also want to be available to address the specific needs of black families who have decided to homeschool or are considering it. While home education is gathering more supporters in the black community, the option is still not fully understood and is often met with strong resistance. These support groups provide much-needed educational and emotional support to black families who have taken the step to educate their children at home. . . .

Though we don't believe that public education is wrong for all black children, we know from our own experience, and from the experiences of other black families, that there are other ways of learning. Many black families across the nation are finding this to be true, and I'm sure others will as well. Now, as our daughters grow and learn every day, Michael and I are even more convinced that we have made the right choice for our family and for our daughters' educational futures. We have equipped them with a true and unwavering love for learning that has been made possible by homeschooling.

Homeschooling Enables a Rightly Ordered Life

Sally Thomas

Sally Thomas is a poet and a contributor to the monthly journal First Things: A Journal of Religion, Culture, and Public Life.

W<sup>e had gone to dinner with old friends, and in the course of the evening the conversation turned to our home-schooling. Our hosts didn't want to argue with the decision my husband and I had made to homeschool; in truth, people do that a lot less often than we had steeled ourselves to expect early on. I suppose they didn't ask how we expected our children to be "socialized" because there the children were, in front of everyone, doing their best impersonations of socialized people. The nine-year-old talked to the grownups about *Star Wars*, the four-year-old helped to carry dishes to the table, the three-year-old played nicely on the floor with our friends' baby granddaughter. The twelve-year-old, away at a ballet rehearsal, proclaimed her socialization by her absence.

In fact, our friends' questions had nothing to do with the welfare of our children, because they could see for themselves that the children were fine. But they were curious, and what they wanted to know was simply this: *What do you do all day long?*

Efficiency and Effectiveness

That's never an easy question to answer. When people think of school, typically they think of a day dominated by a roster of discrete subjects. In English, you do reading, writing, spelling, and grammar. In math, you do numbers. In history, you do what's been done before.

In our homeschool, though we cover all these necessary subjects, the delineations between subjects are often far from clear. For example, this fall my math-tutor brother gave us a book entitled *Famous Mathematicians*, a series of little biographies beginning with Euclid and ending with Norbert Wiener in the twentieth century. The nine-year-old asked if he could read it, so twice a week, during our math time, instead of doing regular computational math, I let him read. When he finished the book, he chose one famous mathematician to profile and wrote a little report. As I was describing this exercise for our friends, I kept thinking that we had either done an awful lot of math and given English the short end of the stick, or else had done a lot of English and shafted math. But then I realized that in fact we had done it all. He had learned math concepts, he had learned history, he had practiced reading and writing and spelling and editing—all by reading one book and writing about it.

At home we can do what's nearly impossible in a school setting.

In recent years, as homeschooling has moved closer to the mainstream, much has been said about the successes of homeschooled children, especially regarding their statistically superior performance on standardized tests and the attractiveness of their transcripts and portfolios to college-admissions boards. Less, I think, has been said about how and why these successes happen. The fact is that homeschooling is an efficient way to teach and learn. It's time-effective, in that a homeschooled child, working independently or one-on-one with a parent or an older sibling, can get through more work or master a concept more quickly than a child who's one of twenty-five in a classroom. It's effort-effective, in that a child doesn't spend needless hours over a concept already mastered simply because others haven't mastered it yet. Conversely, a child doesn't spend years in school quietly not learning a subject, under the teacher's radar, only to face the massive and depressing task of remediation when the deficiency is finally caught.

Interweaving Learning and Life

To my mind, however, homeschooling's greatest efficiency lies in its capacity for a rightly ordered life. A child in school almost inevitably has a separate existence, a "school life," that too easily weakens parental authority and values and that also encourages an artificial boundary between *learning* and *everything else*. Children come home exhausted from a day at school—and for a child with working parents, that day can be twelve hours long—and the last thing they want is to pick up a book or have a conversation. Television and video games demand relatively little, and they seem a blessed departure from what the children have been doing all day. "You know I don't read all that stuff you read," a neighbor child scornfully told my eldest some years ago during one of those archetypal childhood arguments about what to play. Our daughter wanted to play *Treasure-Seekers* or *Betsy-Tacy* and *Tib* [based on characters from books]; her friend insisted on playing the Disney cartoon character Kim Possible. Book-talk was for school, and she wasn't at school just then, thank you.

Our days are saturated with what school merely strives to replicate: real, substantial, active, useful, and moral learning.

At home we can do what's nearly impossible in a school setting: We can weave learning into the fabric of our family life, so that the lines between "learning" and "everything else" have largely ceased to exist. The older children do a daily schedule of what I call sit-down work: math lessons, English and foreign-language exercises, and readings for history and science. The nine-year-old does roughly two hours of sit-down work a day, while the twelve-year-old spends three to four hours. But those hours hardly constitute the sum total of their education.

We spend some time formally learning Latin, for example, but we also say our table blessing in Latin and sing Latin hymns during prayers. Both older children sing in our parish treble choir: still more Latin, which is not a dead language to them but a living, singing one. The twelve-year-old is working her way through an English-grammar-and-composition text, but she is also, on her own, writing a play, which our local children's theater will produce in the spring. The nine-year-old has his own subscription to *National Geographic* and fills us in at dinner on the events of the D-Day invasion or the habits of the basking shark. He practices handwriting, with which he struggles, by writing letters to friends in England, where we lived when he was small. Last November, the older children and a friend adopted a project for sending care packages to soldiers in Iraq; they wrote letters, knitted hats, made Christmas cards, and one Saturday went door-to-door around the neighborhood collecting funds to cover postage and to buy school supplies for the soldiers to hand out to Iraqi children. This undertaking by itself was something of a mini-curriculum, involving reading, handwriting, composition, art, math, community service, and even public relations. At their best, our days are saturated with what school merely strives to replicate: real, substantial, active, useful and moral learning.

Faith and Learning Integrated

Most important for us in the ordering of our life is that our homeschooling day unfolds from habits of prayer. We begin the day with the rosary and a saint's life; we say the Angelus at lunchtime; we do a lesson from the catechism or a reading in apologetics and say the evening office [prayers usually only said by professional religious] before bed. Our children have internalized this rhythm and, to my intense gratification, the older children marshal the younger children to prayers even when their father and I are absent. The day is shaped and organized by times of turning to God.

A lot of unscheduled learning seems to happen during these times. In saying the rosary, for example, we exercise our skills in memorization and recitation, as well as in contemplation. The little children practice sitting still; they also practice counting. In remembering our daily intentions together, we practice the discipline of inclining our hearts and minds toward the needs of others. Often, too, during devotions we find ourselves plunged into discussions about current events, ethics, and questions about God and life that have been simmering unasked in some child's mind until just that moment. The saints, whose dates we record in our family timeline book, provide us not only with examples of holiness but also with insight into the historical eras in which they lived. We have even found ourselves doing geography during prayers. . . .

What looks like not that much on the daily surface of things proves in the living to be something greater than the schedule on the page suggests, a life in which English and math and science and history, contemplation and discussion and action, faith and learning, are not compartmentalized entities but elements in an integrated whole from which, we hope and pray, our children will emerge one day so firmly formed that nothing in this world can unbend them.

Homeschooling Allows Parents to Teach Their Religious Convictions

Mark Field and Christine Field

Mark Field is a former lieutenant in United States Naval Intelligence and the Wheaton, Illinois, chief of police. Christine Field is senior correspondent and Resource Room columnist for The Old Schoolhouse Magazine *and the author of several books, including* Homeschooling the Challenging Child. *Together the Fields authored* Homeschooling 101: The Essential Handbook.

If we hadn't chosen homeschooling, we don't think our marriage would be as strong as it is, with the range and depth of experiences we have had. Without the calling to homeschool, we would not have the shared commitment to the ultimate home improvement project—homeschooling. While other couples may only get to share decorating projects and vacation decisions, we struggle together through everything from salvation to phonics to algebra. . . .

If we hadn't chosen homeschooling, we probably wouldn't have as many children, Christine practiced law until our first child was two years old and our second child was six months old. The siren call of an engaging career was strong and might have won out. If not for the happy arrival of two children seventeen months apart in age and the opportunity for a dream job in a distant city for Mark, we might not have abandoned our status as dual-income parents. Christine's time at home was supposed to be short lived. "The plan" was to be home for a few years, then reenter the courtroom arena. However God had another plan—to adopt two more children, bringing the total to four. The move from a prestigious comfort zone to home was the values clarifying experience that we both needed. . . .

Educating a Family Is Challenging

If we hadn't chosen homeschooling, we would know the hollowness of having more "things" but never know the richness of having all of each other. Many times we are tempted to lament our lifestyle of relative simplicity. We need only look at the many upwardly mobile families we know who are blessed materially, but bankrupt spiritually. . . .

If we hadn't chosen homeschooling, we might not have experienced our own much needed time on God's threshing floor. The challenges of raising and educating a family have been met on our knees, which was exactly where the Lord wanted us. Any vestige of pride or self-sufficiency that lurked in our desperately wicked hearts has been exposed by the rigors of this life. . . .

If we hadn't chosen homeschooling, we doubt our children would be as close as they are. As different as night and day, they are capable of shining moments of closeness and bonding. The tenderness (and sometimes the terror!) they bestow on one another causes our parent-hearts to leap. Capable of relating to a wide array of people, they often (not always!) choose to relate most profoundly to those they live with.

Freedom and Space to Explore and Nurture

If we hadn't chosen homeschooling, a foray into teenage rebellion might not have ended so graciously. When one of our brood sought out her birthmother, we prayed for a happy ending, not knowing what to expect. She made contact but got no response, causing our daughter many months of depression, doubt, and distrust. In her pain, she lashed out at us. We loved her through it, and she is now a happy young lady. We shudder to think of the course this incident might have taken if she had been exposed to the sea of adolescent angst and its remedies practiced in the schools. The pain relief she sought might have been found in self-destructive ways. . . .

If we hadn't chosen homeschooling, our children might not have had the time, freedom, and space to explore and nurture personal interests and talents. A passion for swimming, a flair for acting, an untapped talent for watercolor, and much more have all been nurtured in the greenhouse of our home. Schoolwork can be done efficiently, leaving time for other pursuits, or lingered over at our leisure. Nothing fosters self-discovery like freedom.

If we hadn't chosen homeschooling, our daughter with learning issues might not be the strong, wise, compassionate young lady that she is becoming. She could have been beaten down by a system that had no time to explore or appreciate her considerable strengths. Instead, we had the time to learn how to help her learn, and she is flourishing.

If we hadn't chosen homeschooling, our irrepressible son would certainly have been repressed and labeled. He is a busy, busy boy, and we have learned that he is extremely capable. It so happens that he does not learn well with his behind glued to a chair. With our freedom to tailor-make "school" to meet the needs of each child, he is learning while jumping, walking, fiddling, and bouncing. . . .

Christians . . . point to their religious faith as a strong factor in their decision to teach their children at home.

The Factor of Religious Faith

And we haven't even touched on the academic advantages.

The goal of our homeschooling is to prepare our children for a life dedicated to God—seeking his will, seeking to glorify him. This is in contrast to a culture drowning in secular humanism that says to glorify ourselves.

In schools, children are statistical entities to justify funding. In the homeschool, they are precious sacred trusts. The world doesn't need more geniuses or star athletes or beauty queens. It needs more committed, passionate Christians.

Statistics show that the overwhelming majority of American homeschoolers are Christians who point to their religious faith as a strong factor in their decision to teach their children at home. Somewhere along the line, each of these families first heard a calling, and hearing that calling set the stage for how their homeschooling would unfurl. Only fully understanding that calling will lead to peace and confidence. . . .

Knowing and Shaping Children's Hearts

If loving God and teaching our children about him is to be our first priority, we must first shape our children's hearts, not their minds. What does this mean? Allow me to employ a time-honored methodology cherished by ministers and teachers the world over: the acrostic—HEART.

As homeschoolers we have the distinct advantage of one-on-one interaction with our students.

H Is for Hearts. We must know our children's hearts and do all we can to ensure they are inclined heavenward. This is of far greater worth to us than a prestigious prep school or a perfect SAT score. Unless we have their hearts, their trust, and their obedience, we cannot teach them anything. But if we have their hearts, and if they will listen to God's rebuke, he will pour out his heart to us and make his thoughts known to them. . . . That, friend, is true education: the pouring of God's heart (and our hearts) into our children.

E Is for Eternity. We believe homeschooling is the best education for our children because it is education with an eye on eternity. We had a discussion about public school versus homeschooling with a Christian brother a while back. At the time he was the principal of a respected suburban high school. He noted that the facilities of our humble homeschool could not hold a candle to the high-powered microscopes that allowed his students to see the internal workings of a human cell. True, I said, we don't have the bells and whistles you find at a well-funded public school, but we are able to meet the individual needs of each of our students. We can teach them the way that they best learn, and we can instill in them a vision for eternity. . . .

The homeschool environment is simply more conducive than public school for helping our children pursue right relationships and a well-rounded social life.

A Is for Attitude and Abilities. As homeschoolers we have the distinct advantage of one-on-one interaction with our students. This allows us to recognize and work on bad attitudes and to encourage a child's unique abilities. In a large classroom setting a child can fly under the radar for years without anyone ever knowing he has a poor attitude toward learning, toward life, toward people. In the homeschool environment, such attitudes will be readily apparent and can be dealt with on a daily basis. Meanwhile, the child is not continually exposed to the dishonoring attitudes so prevalent in the public schools, where basic manners seem to have gone the way of the horse and buggy.

In addition to shaping attitude, we can foster a child's unique abilities. Homeschooling affords us the precious freedom to craft courses to the child's interests and to pursue activities outside of school that meet his or her needs.

R Is for Right Relationships. The homeschool environment is simply more conducive than public school for helping our children pursue right relationships and a well-rounded social life. For example, our days do not consist merely of academic pursuits in the home. The children interact with people of all ages, from all walks of life, whether through group activities with other homeschoolers, specialized lessons outside the home, or volunteer opportunities. Regular exposure to all age groups develops in a child the ability to communicate with anyone and to relate to everyone. In addition, we can keep our fingers on the pulse of family dynamics, friendships, and boy-girl relationships. A good deal of socializing is done in our home where we can observe interactions and talk about them, on the spot or later in private. An environment that allows for this type of life coaching is priceless.

T Is for Today and Tomorrow. We cherish today and relish the thought of tomorrow. We have precious few todays left until our children leave the nest, so we want to "suck out all the marrow of life" while we are still together. Meanwhile, homeschooling allows us to look to that tomorrow with joyous hope. We pray the normal prayers of parents—spiritual health, life purpose, a godly mate, college, career, children—but we rest in the knowledge that we have made wise investments of our resources, time, and talents as parents and that God holds our children's future in the palm of his hands.

Homeschooling Provides the Best Education

W.A. Pannapacker

W.A. Pannapacker is an associate professor of English at Hope College in Holland, Michigan.

I'm an English professor, and my spouse used to work in academic administration. We have three daughters, ages 6, 4, and 2. And we have been home schooling them for two years now. If all goes well, we plan to continue teaching them at home at least until they are old enough for high school.

We always planned that one of us would stay home while our children were young, but the idea of home schooling only developed recently in the context of our present circumstances.

A Natural Method of Education

Teaching our daughters to read and write, beginning around the age of 4, seemed like a natural thing for us to do. Along with potty training, it was just part of the ordinary business of being a parent. Being avid readers ourselves, we have about 4,000 books in our house, which now includes a children's library. I suppose it was inevitable that we would spend a lot of time reading to our children, and they would have an early desire to learn to read for themselves and for each other.

We live surrounded by woods and farmland, so our daughters are constantly asking us to look up plants and insects in the Audubon field guides. We have a reasonably well-supplied children's science lab and art studio. And, in the course of routine travel and shopping, it's easy to cultivate our daughters' curiosity about the world by visiting museums,

W.A. Pannapacker, "Children, the Case for Homeschooling," *Chronicle of Higher Education*, December 16, 2005. This article may not be published, reposted, or redistributed without express permission from The Chronicle.

zoos, libraries, schools, factories, and farms. These are things that most parents do, though they may not regard their activities as part of some kind of curriculum.

We want the best education for our children, and, on the whole, home schooling seems like the best option.

In a typical day, our 6-year-old daughter will study phonics, spelling, writing, history, geography, and math. She may perform some elementary science experiments, or she may work on an art project in emulation of [artists George Pierre] Seurat or [Jackson] Pollock. On some days other children— not necessarily other home schoolers—will come to our house to play. Sometimes they'll open our costume chest and dramatize something they've been reading, such as *The Hobbit*. Other times they'll go outside and play hide-and-seek or go on an "expedition" to find specimens for the family museum. Even though our younger daughters have not yet started their formal schooling, they are eager to imitate their oldest sister, and the pace of learning seems to accelerate with each new child. On good days, home schooling seems like the most natural method of elementary education one could imagine.

Home schooling . . . becomes a logical choice when the costs of private education and day care become greater than one parent's income.

We are not ideologically committed to home schooling any more than we are opposed to public education. And we are aware of the limitations of home under some circumstances, just as we are aware of the difficulties faced by many public schools, even in relatively well-financed school districts. Ultimately, we want the best education for our children, and, on the whole, home schooling seems like the best option. It is also one that our daughters seem to desire, and, if any of them wanted to go to the nearby public school, we would certainly consider it. . . .

Private Education Is Not the Answer

I have had many discussions with other professors who home school, primarily at my home institution but also with a number of faculty members in other parts of the country. From those conversations I have noticed a number of common motives, circumstances, and beliefs among faculty members who educate their children at home.

They are rarely religious or political extremists. Many professors observe that it is difficult to achieve consistent moral training in public education. They sometimes state that private education in religious schools is too doctrinal or resistant to modernity, particularly in the sciences. Some lament that public and religious education seem to have become battlefields for activists for whom the "vital center" has been abandoned, along with a spirit of civic responsibility.

They want the best education for their children, but they are not wealthy. Professors are usually well informed about what constitutes a good education in terms of methods and resources. The experience of small classes and one-on-one tutoring inevitably convinces teachers of the effectiveness of methods that can easily be replicated in the home, though they are prohibitive for all but exclusive private schools that are usually beyond the reach of academics with more than one child. Home schooling therefore, becomes a logical choice when the costs of private education and day care become greater than one parent's income.

They enjoy learning. For nearly all professors, the chance to review and expand their own youthful education in a variety of fields is a treat that almost transcends the educational needs of their children. Mathematicians, for example, relish the chance to reread the literature they half-missed when they were mastering geometry, and English professors, like me, enjoy the chance to relearn the astronomy they once loved before [failing to grasp] calculus crushed their hopes for a scientific career. They often see themselves as learning with their children rather than simply teaching them.

Confidence and Flexibility Are Key

They are confident in their ability to teach. Professors often see teaching their own children as part of a continuum of pleasurable obligations to the next generation; they seek to integrate the values of their profession with the values they live at home. Since professors often teach the teachers, they tend to believe—perhaps with some hubris—in their ability to teach effectively at all grade levels. But more often, they recognize their limitations and seek collaboration with other parents— often professors themselves—with different areas of expertise.

Home-schooled students are not always perfect, but they seem more respectful, attentive, mature, and academically prepared than their peers.

They benefit from flexible schedules. Academics tend to work about 50 hours per week during the academic year, but they also have control over their schedules and long periods of relative autonomy. Most professors have a co-parenting ideal, but in practice one partner—usually the mother—becomes the primary home educator, while the father assumes a secondary role with some seasonal variation. Some express discomfort with this circumstance because they recognize the sacrifices that each partner requires of the other.

They value unstructured learning. Professors know how much time is lost by learning in an institutional setting. A large portion of the time spent in school is devoted to moving students around, dealing with disruptions, health problems, different amounts of preparation, and unequal rates of learning. Without all the crowd control and level seeking, the formal requirements of education can be completed in only a few hours a day, leaving lots of time for self-directed learning and play. As a result, home schooled children generally learn faster and with less boredom and less justified resentment.

School sometimes teaches otherwise happy and intelligent children to become sullen and secretive and contemptuous of learning.

Negative Side of Public Education

They see the results of public education. Every professor seems to complain that most high-school graduates are not really prepared for college, either academically or emotionally. More and more, our energies are devoted to remedial teaching and therapeutic counseling. Most believe that something is wrong in public education, or the larger culture, that can only be dealt with, in part, by selective withdrawal. Home schooled students are not always perfect, but they seem more respectful, attentive, mature, and academically prepared than their peers. And they do not automatically perceive teachers as "the enemy" out of peer solidarity.

They privilege the family over peer groups. Professors often celebrate diversity as a value in education, and, among those who home school, many mention the value for their children of cross-generational experiences instead of identifying only with a peer group. In large families, children also benefit from teaching their younger siblings, who are generally eager to keep up. Home schooled students are less likely to become alienated from their families as a result of antisocial, anti-intellectual peer conformity. They develop a set of values that enables them to resist the negative socialization that outweighs, by far, the benefits of segregation by age.

They have negative memories of their own education. Although it takes some probing, nearly every professor with home schooled children mentions traumatic childhood experiences in school. Professors, as a group, tend to have been sensitive, intelligent children who were picked on and ostracized. They foresee the same treatment for their own children, and they want to do everything they can to prevent the children from experiencing the traumas they experienced. Professors recognize how many of our most brilliant students have been emotionally or physically terrorized for a dozen years before they arrive at college. School sometimes teaches otherwise happy and intelligent children to become, sullen and secretive and contemptuous of learning.

Worth the Sacrifices

It is hard to overemphasize this last point as a motive for home schoolers. In my own memory, the difficulty of school was never the work; it was surviving the day without being victimized by students whose violence was beyond the capacity or desire of adults to control. My spouse remembers the cruelty of girls in cliques, who can be even more cunning at the infliction of pain and permanent emotional scarring than any of the boys who sometimes sent me home with torn clothes and a bloody nose.

No doubt, my spouse and I have had to forgo some career options for our present way of life. Home schooling our children means we have to live on an assistant professor's salary. It also means living in a small town in the Midwest instead of an expensive city on one of the coasts. It means living in an old farmhouse that I am, more or less, renovating by myself. It means not eating out or going on vacations very often. It means driving older American cars instead of shiny new Volvos. But the big reward is the time we get to spend with our children.

I suppose, on some level, my spouse and I are rebelling against an academic culture that tells us we should both be working at demanding professional jobs while our children are raised by someone else. But we value this time with our children more than career advancement for its own sake. We don't regard ourselves as conservatives. We feel like we're swimming against the mainstream of a culture that has sacrificed the family for economic productivity and personal ambition. We don't think home schooling is right for everyone, but it works for us, for now. Of course we will make some mistakes, but on the whole, we think home schooling our children may be the most important thing we will ever do.

Homeschooled Children Learn Life Lessons

Christina Rosales

Christina Rosales is a reporter for the Laredo Morning Times *in Laredo, Texas.*

Hannah sits at her school desk in the brightly colored classroom, her legs swinging from her perch on the chair, her feet teasing the floor she can't reach yet.

As the first-grader reads her story from her book, "Mouse Soup," her voice and eyebrows express the differences between the character dialogue and the narrator.

"Sound it out, Hannah," said Toni Migura, her mother and schoolteacher. "Remember what the phonogram for A–I is. This word (mountain) breaks the rule." "M-ow-n-tAN," Hannah reads.

"Very good, baby girl," Migura said.

Incorporating Life Lessons

As ... students embark on the new school year—some worrying about mandatory uniforms, class schedules and test scores—homeschool students like Hannah and her brother, Matthew, head back to their familiar, homey classrooms.

"I love homeschool," said Matthew Migura, a fourth-grader. "The thing I like best is that my mom is my teacher, and that my dog can come into my classroom when I call him." Toni Migura said she, as well as several other homeschool parents, choose to homeschool their kids to teach life lessons and character.

"No matter what we're doing, we put life lessons into what they're learning," she said. "We're always teaching about patience and manners. You're able to teach a lot about character." Aside from instructing their children in virtues, the Miguras choose to homeschool their children to incorporate a Christian education.

"We want them to be educated," Migura said. "But above all, we want them to grow up to be godly men and women." Dominic and Nicole Vallone, parents who homeschool their three children, begin the school day with Bible study. Their three children, Duncan, 8, Nolan, 6 and Asher, 4 are all taught about their faith as Christians.

A Focus on Firm Education

"My mom and dad homeschool us because other schools don't have God in them," said Duncan Vallone, a fourth-grader. "They don't want us to go off and become non-believers in the end." Both Toni Migura and Nicole Vallone encourage their children to question their faith and why they believe.

We want them to have a very firm foundation and know how to learn and have a love of learning.

For example, Vallone said, the Christian curriculum used does not teach evolution as fact.

"I do teach them evolution in an apologetic way, but we're creationists," she said. "I want them to be able to defend their faith when they get to college and people ask them questions and debate those types of issues." The primary goal of homeschooling for the Vallones and Miguras is not for their children to get ahead, they said.

"We're not trying to make them into geniuses," Nicole Vallone said. "I do want them to be well-rounded, but that's not my first desire."

Dominic Vallone and Toni Migura said [that] with the children getting the attention they need, learning is easier for the students. "When you have them one-on-one, you can cater to their strengths and talents," Dominic Vallone said. "Their academic success is really a product of that." Toni Migura's focus when homeschooling Hannah and Matthew is to give them a firm foundation in their education.

Socialization Is an Everyday Happening

"It's not so they're ahead of the game," she said. "We want them to have a very firm foundation and know how to learn and have a love of learning. Once they have that, they can apply it to anything they want to do." While some people believe that homeschooled children may not be properly socialized, the Migura and Vallone children are very much in tune with their peers.

Hannah and Matthew take karate and piano lessons, and keep busy with their friends from church and the neighborhood, Migura said.

"They (Duncan, Nolan and Asher) have many friends," Nicole Vallone said. "There are always friends here at the house, and as they get older, we'll have them do golf camps and other things." In addition to their after-school activities, the Vallones and the Miguras are members of the Providence Homeschool Association, a Christian support group for homeschool families.

The group consists of about 50 families, said Dominic Vallone, one of the leaders of the group. Providence organizes monthly field trips for homeschool students, as well as annual science and history fairs.

That's what homeschool is about—accepting that sometimes plans and schedules don't work out.

Flexibility Is the Key

Homeschool isn't for everyone, Dominic Vallone said.

"There are a lot of different ways to educate kids," he said. "For us, homeschool is the best way to instill goals and character in our children." Duncan and Nolan Vallone said their friends, most of whom will go back to school on Monday, consider the boys lucky.

"I like that I don't have to sit in class all day," Duncan said. "I could take breaks." The Miguras, depending on the kind of day it is outside, sometimes take the whole day off.

"Sometimes we have those nice spring days and I'll say 'No school today,'" Migura said. "We'll spend the day outside or go to the library. It teaches you to appreciate the day. That's what homeschool is about—accepting that sometimes plans and schedules don't work out." Most homeschool families follow a curriculum purchased through different publishers.

The Importance of Teaching Character and Faith

Unlike the public school system, classes for the Vallones don't end until the curriculum is done Nicole said; the classes could extend into the first few weeks of summer.

Asked if he would rather go to school with his friends, Nolan, a first grader said he would rather be homeschooled.

"Not even my mom and dad have to stop me," he said.

People often ask what the motivation is for these families who have never sent their children to a school, Migura said.

"People sometimes think we're crazy," she said. "But the goal of all of this is to teach more than the curriculum . . . [including] character and faith. It's more than getting through the textbook."

Homeschooling Benefits Special Needs Children

Meg Grooms

Meg Grooms is the homeschooling editor for BellaOnline, a women's Web site.

Every single child in this world is different and has different educational needs. Parents who have children with special education needs face unique challenges. I happen to have two special needs children who are homeschooled. The good news is that homeschooling your special needs child is often the best situation for the child, and your child doesn't have to give up school-funded therapies in order to homeschool, and it doesn't have to hurt your wallet. The hard work of homeschooling a special needs child is twice as rewarding.

Eligible for Outside Help

Most states allow children to be evaluated for special programs at the public school, including students who do the bulk of their learning outside of a traditional school. Homeschooled children in most states are eligible to receive free speech therapy, autism support, occupational therapy, gifted education and other programs through their locally zoned public school. Your child will attend school for these programs only; they do not need to be enrolled full-time. Using this option is generally the least expensive and most convenient for a family; however family participation isn't always encouraged and you may find yourself fighting to stay informed of your child's status. You may also feel pressure from the school to enroll your child full-time. If this happens remember that they are speaking from a numbers and funding standpoint; schools garner three times as much funding for

Meg Grooms, "Special Needs Homeschooling," *bellaonline.com*, 2008. Reproduced by permission.

special education students as they do "normal" students. Your local school district will have all of the information you need to have your child evaluated, and you generally do not have to have a prior evaluation or referral from a doctor. The school has a legal obligation to provide these services to your child regardless of where your child is educated. If you find the program just isn't working out you are free to remove your child at any time to seek services elsewhere.

Many private and church schools have programs for special needs children at a reduced cost, including autism support programs several days a week.

Most states also offer early interventions programs for children identified before the age of 5 as having special needs. In some states these programs work hand-in-hand with the local schools, but since all are publicly funded they are open to *all* children who qualify.

Evaluations, programs and therapies will be provided at no cost, and many can be performed in your home. A quick call to your state's Department of Health should gain you all the information you need to get your child evaluated.

Private Insurance Offers Alternatives

Parents who have private medical insurance might be surprised at what they will pay for. Many top-tier insurance plans now cover speech therapy, hearing aids, physical therapy, psychological care, occupational therapy and many other therapies and programs your child can benefit from. There are hoops that you will have to jump through, and you will most likely need the referral of a physician. This is a wonderful alternative for those who are unable to take their children to a school for these services or who want to try to keep everything in-house and under the radar. While this option is not free, it is desirable for those in the position to pay for therapy and who want the government school system involved as little as possible. If your family participates in a state-funded insurance program you are eligible for these services through your state Department of Health at no cost in most cases. When your child reaches compulsory school attendance age you will be referred to the local school district for most services. If you do not have insurance most hospitals that offer these services have a sliding scale, some have limited amounts of state funding to cover the costs of low income and uninsured children.

There are alternative service locations available if you know where to look. In many communities tutoring for all ages is offered for free or low cost at senior centers, community centers, churches and church schools, the YMCA and other community clubs, community colleges and universities. Many private and church schools have programs for special needs children at a reduced cost, including autism support programs several days a week.

Special Needs Children Benefit from Homeschooling

While homeschooling a special needs child takes more effort than homeschooling a child who doesn't need these services, you are your child's best advocate and you have the ultimate choice of where and how their education will take place.

- Your child doesn't need to go to school in order to receive the services they need.

- It is your job as parent to ensure your children get the best possible education, and for most special needs students traditional school isn't the best option, and it is certainly not the only option.

- Arm yourself with information and surround yourself with people who care and can support you. Locate a support group geared for parents of special education children who are homeschooled, research the Internet, talk to professionals and make a sound decision based on your information and child.

CHAPTER 2

Is Homeschooling a Good Option?

Chapter Preface

Most experts agree that homeschooling has become the fastest growing option for parents thinking about alternative education and school choice for their children. Yet, despite this, many people remain undecided as to whether or not homeschool is the best choice for today's youth.

One of the strongest critics of homeschooling is the National Education Association (NEA), which has taken the position that "home schooling programs based on parental choice cannot provide the student with a comprehensive education experience." Others point out that some parents are not qualified to teach; in other words, they are not knowledgeable enough or have not been trained sufficiently to do the job. Anyone, argued one member of the Illinois Education Association, can buy a social studies, science, or math book, but that does not mean that person knows how to instruct someone else about the subject matter contained in that book. Homeschool critics and skeptics also contend that most parents cannot create a full learning experience because they do not have easy access to the wide variety of resources readily available to classroom teachers.

On a par with concern about teacher certification or accreditation is concern about whether children who are homeschooled are subject to a lack of socialization. At one time or another, almost every homeschool parent has been asked, "What about socialization?" Socialization is an important component of getting along in life, goes the argument. You cannot teach it.

The NEA believes that children should have the opportunity to interact with their peers and others in order to develop physically and mentally, expand social skills, and acclimate to new people and surroundings. In the view of the NEA and of others who do not favor homeschooling or are uncertain about its merits, this interaction is what happens when children attend an academic institution. In a school environment, they say, children not only learn how to communicate with their peers, but also to respect those different from themselves and to work as a team to accomplish goals.

Some homeschoolers and homeschooling advocates refer to socialization as the "dreaded S word" and to the issue as the "Socialization Myth." They agree with homeschooling critics that socialization is extremely important. They do not agree, however, that children who are homeschooled are isolated, confined, or lacking in social skills. Homeschoolers, they explain, are involved in numerous extracurricular activities that enable them to spend time and interact with people of all ages and types.

Writing for About.com, Jennie von Eggers, author and co-owner of Trigger Memory Systems, a publishing company that focuses on creative learning, responded this way to assertions that homeschoolers could not integrate well into society because they lacked opportunities to learn and practice social skills:

"How would my children be able to integrate into society, without first learning the valuable "social skills" that only a public school experience could provide? After all, the socialization part of a typical day-in-the-life of a home schooled child, looks nothing like the government school experience. Many homeschoolers spend their day doing things such as: helping out with family business, running errands, going on field trips, visiting relatives and friends, doing odd jobs for neighbors and partaking in family responsibilities. As the "socially challenged" homeschool kids are out and about, partaking and interacting in real life situations, the government students are "socializing" under a controlled environment, behind four walls with a controlled group of people (also known as their peer group)."

Another parent, this time speaking to those who home-school, makes it clear that homeschoolers will indeed be socialized and able to function in society: "Your homeschooled kids will have as many friends and activities as they want and you allow (and likely more time than their PS [public school] peers to enjoy them). They will be socialized by their parents and other caring people who will help them learn appropriate behavior in different situations—at home, in public, in informal and formal activities."

Homeschool advocates believe strongly that children do not have to go to public school to be truly socialized. Some experts agree. One of these is Terry Osborn, professor and chair of the Division of Curriculum and Teaching at Fordham University's Graduate School of Education, who is quoted in the following excerpt from a January 21, 2008, posting on MySA.com titled "Home-Schooling Doesn't Stunt Kids' Socialization:"

"The idea of a homogenous grouping of 25 to 30 children who sit at their desks all day long and do activities—to call that socialization is tortured. You and I don't live and function in that kind of environment." Socialization involves interacting with people from various backgrounds in various contexts, and most home-schooled kids do that, he says. "Interacting with adults in the grocery store is a form of socialization," he adds. Many home-schooled kids have siblings of different ages, and that affords cross-generational socializing, which students don't get at school. As long as parents make an effort to expand the child's circle beyond the home, home-schooled kids do fine, he says. "Socialization isn't rocket science, after all," Osborn says. "When you go off to college you learn pretty fast when to speak and when not to speak."

Homeschooling Works Better than Traditional Public Education

Kate McReynolds

Kate McReynolds is a child clinical psychologist and the associate editor of Encounter *magazine.*

Across the nation, public schools are cutting back or eliminating recess, art, music, physical education, and drama. Excessive homework and test-prep are encroaching on children's free time and family time, making it difficult for them to engage in activities that are important for their full development. Competitive college entrance requirements push young people to take Advanced Placement courses and SAT-prep courses, adding to their already heavy homework loads. The school work itself, driven by high-stakes tests, is typically dull and lifeless, consisting of little besides the memorization of disembodied facts and concepts. Children seem to dislike school more than ever.

We are told that all this is necessary to prepare our children for the future. But is it? Is there an alternative way to educate our children that will respect their happiness and individuality, and will foster their natural love of learning? Growing numbers of parents are turning to homeschooling.

By its very nature, homeschooling cannot be easily described. There is no unified homeschool "movement," no standardized curriculum or centralized source of information on academic achievement. Parents have many different reasons for homeschooling their children. For some the motivation is not the repressive and dreary nature of the public school cur-

Kate McReynolds, "Homeschooling," *Encounter*, vol. 20, Summer 2007, pp. 36–41. Reprinted with permission from Encounter: Education for Meaning and Social Justice. https://great-ideas.org/enc.htm.

riculum, but the need to teach a religious-based education. Other parents fear violence in the schools. Still others want to spend more time with their children.

Homeschoolers attend college at higher rates than public school students.

Some homeschooled children follow a traditional curriculum and a set schedule, some are "deschooled," a style of homeschooling that permits children to follow their own interests at their own pace. Some homeschoolers engage in "distance learning," i.e., Internet-based instruction, and purchase books and ready-made curricula. Many make or find their own materials, join learning cooperatives, and make use of community-based learning opportunities, such as public lectures, community theater, and continuing education classes. Increasingly, homeschoolers are joining together to share resources and even to form partnerships with traditional schools. But regardless of the form it takes, homeschooling is a growing trend, increasing annually by 15 to 20 percent.

Evaluating the Outcomes

Academic achievement among U.S. homeschoolers is difficult to assess. There is no uniform curriculum; standardized tests are voluntary in many states; and federal systems of "accountability" are absent. Nevertheless, a variety of studies suggest that by traditional standards, homeschoolers do pretty well. They tend to score higher than public school children on standardized achievement tests, advanced placement exams, the SAT and the ACT. Homeschoolers attend college at higher rates than public school students.

About three-quarters of the nation's colleges have policies regarding homeschool applicants and many, including Harvard, actively recruit homeschoolers. In 2001 Stanford University admitted 27% of its homeschooled applicants, nearly twice the acceptance rate of traditionally schooled applicants. Once in college homeschoolers tend to have higher grade point averages than their traditionally schooled peers.

I knew something was wrong on the first day of school.

Despite its apparent academic success, a prevalent mainstream concern is that homeschooling deprives children of the social and emotional development necessary to make it in the "real" world. The socialization question, as it is often called, represents a number of concerns. If children don't attend traditional schools will they be able to cope with college? Will they be able to get and keep a job? Will homeschooled children know how to get along with others? Will they tolerate people's differences? Will they know how to behave as society expects? I decided to talk with homeschoolers to get a better idea of their day-to-day life.

From Apathy to Enthusiasm

Ellen, who lives in Brooklyn, New York, homeschools her five children. She was originally somewhat opposed to homeschooling, put off by her impression that homeschoolers were trying to shield themselves from the world, but all that changed when she sent Aidan, her first child, to kindergarten. "I knew something was wrong on the first day of school. I asked the teacher if I could meet with her and she seemed shocked. She agreed, but during our meeting her attitude seemed to be, 'What are you doing here?'" Although the school, which Ellen had researched and carefully selected, had an open door policy, Aidan's teacher didn't value parent cooperation. There were 37 children in Aidan's class and they were expected to sit in desks and do academic worksheets; there was very little playtime. Aidan, who already knew how to read, was bored and restless. Ellen was surprised to get reports that her well-behaved son was acting up in school. She discovered that the punishment was losing recess, which struck her as counterproductive. At home, her young son talked about teachers yelling at students, about students yelling, and about his feeling that his teacher was always watching him. Ellen suspected he had been pegged as a troublemaker. Six weeks into the school year a family emergency required Ellen's attention. She left town for two weeks, taking Aidan with her. When they returned, Aidan did not go back to school.

Ellen is a proponent of Waldorf education, developed by Rudolph Steiner, a holistic developmental approach that discourages introducing academics too early. Aidan spent his first year of homeschool primarily playing with friends, going to the library, doing art, and going on outings with his mother. Now, with five homeschoolers ranging in age from 3 to 13, some of the work is more academic, some of the time more structured. The children learn with books and workbooks, with friends, from programs at the Brooklyn Botanical Gardens, the Museum of Natural History, and other community resources. But each one has a unique developmental path that homeschooling is fostering. . . .

Ellen has been "methodical" about math but, in keeping with her philosophy, does not introduce it too soon.

> I observe my children very carefully to see how things are affecting them, not to cater to their every whim, but to make sure of healthy growth in every aspect of their lives, not just academics. It takes a lot of attention.

It seems to be working. When Ellen's daughter, Justine, who is sunny, artistic, and loving, was six, she spent the entire year drawing pictures. It was all she wanted to do and she was very focused and content. Now 8 years old, her interest is turning to academic subjects and she recently asked for a math workbook. When her mother gave her one shortly before bed-time, Justine took it to bed with her and began working out problems. She enthusiastically told her mother, "Don't be surprised if you see me here in the morning still working."

Ellen believes that by allowing children the freedom to develop their own interests and learn material when they are ready we are protecting their natural enthusiasm and preparing them in the best possible way for the future.

> Their enthusiasm for the things they are interested in is so untainted by competition and external expectations that it's retained. Their enthusiasm for what's coming in the future is preserved. If we expose them to academics too early we're stunting their ability to use their knowledge creatively and in their own way. If it's too early they won't know what to do with what they know, but if we pay attention to the unique way that each child learns and grows, they will be free to accomplish what they want in life.

We are out in the world everyday interacting with people.

The Nonissue of Socialization

Ellen is very familiar with the socialization question. She's puzzled that people think of public school as the "real" world. "It's silly," says Ellen. "This is the world; we all live in it." Ellen believes there are many aspects of traditional schooling that work against healthy socialization, such as age segregation, competition, and the near exclusive focus on academic subjects.

> My children, and other homeschoolers I know, interact with people of all ages. In my family we have to adjust to each individual on a daily basis. There is an awareness of differences, a give and take. The older children help the younger ones and this develops compassion and understanding. Multi-age socializing is a very natural, real world practice that children in traditional schools don't experience. Homeschoolers have more time to socialize too. We are out in the world everyday interacting with people. And the children have time to play with their friends because they're not burdened with afterschool programs and homework.

Ellen goes on to say that cooperation, which she defines as working together for the common good, is not fostered in traditional schools. "How does putting children in a very competitive environment, where the emphasis is on individual achievement, promote social harmony? What are we teaching children when we socialize them in this way?" But Ellen believes that one of the biggest advantages of homeschooling for socializing children is the cultural opportunities it can provide. "The things that we share in our culture, like art and music, are the things that socialize us. This is where we come together as a society. And this is what's being eliminated from public schools."

Ellen's son, Aidan, has decided to start public high school next fall. She's not worried about how he will cope. "This is what *he* wants. He's motivated to be a part of this experience and he's a creative problem solver. He has the skills to overcome whatever challenges he meets."

I'm doing things that really interest me, and that's the cardinal difference.

Fulfillment and Happiness

Elisa is a lively, articulate 15-year-old girl who has been homeschooled for the past year. She is a veteran of the Popcorn School, a parent cooperative pre-K and kindergarten, a public school, and a private school. When the homework started piling up in middle school, Elisa's mother suggested homeschooling. Elisa resisted, fearing she'd become a social outcast. By 8th grade, then in private school, Elisa was doing six hours of homework a night. She was overwhelmed, sleep-deprived, and wanted a break. Desperate, her worries about being a social outcast faded. "I didn't care if I ever saw my friends again." But it took meeting a group of homeschooled children for Elisa to get excited about what she was about to begin. Describing her reaction to a dramatic production that she attended staged by homeschooled children, Elisa said, "These are homeschooled kids and they are happy and they are doing this incredible production. I never looked back." . . .

Elisa told me that she has wanted to write a novel ever since she could say the word "novel." She's writing one now, and studying herbs and medicine. "I'm doing things that really interest me, and that's the cardinal difference. I'm getting to do things that I wouldn't have been able to do in school, things that will help me in my career path and in my life." Elisa also studies French, geography, mathematics, and English. She has two voice teachers and a dance teacher. Elisa and her mother have written a play, a parody of regular school that is currently in production. "It's the most surreal thing about homeschooling. You don't expect to be able to write a play and see actors voicing the words you wrote. It's unbelievably heart-warming and jaw-dropping at the same time."

Did her fears about her social status prove true? Elisa laughs.

> "There are so many misconceptions about homeschoolers, that they're nerds, they're isolated. If you take any class, you'll meet people. But when you choose the classes you take you meet people who are mutually interested, and you come together in a way that you can't in school because in school it's forced down your throat. The people I've met in these classes are friendships I've kept."

Elisa expresses her belief that holistic education is the natural way to learn and that experiential learning is its essence. "Actually getting to touch and feel what you are learning is what's missing in the public schools." She is so wonderfully alive and enthusiastic that I asked Elisa to say more about happiness. She replied:

> This might sound odd, but once when I was little I was at the grocery store with my Dad, I saw this organic milk and on the carton it said, "From happy cows, on happy farms." I

begged my Dad to buy that milk, and I could taste the difference. In schools kids are not naturally grown; they don't develop naturally. They can't tell happy from sad; they are fed emotions. It was a nightmare that I couldn't wake up from. Now I feel real. I feel this is what life should be like. I have never been more fulfilled and genuinely happy. . . .

The World as a Classroom

The stereotype of the isolated, misfit homeschooler is giving way as, in growing numbers, homeschoolers make the world their classroom. It appears that homeschoolers spend more time in their communities and have meaningful interactions with a wider variety of people than traditionally schooled children typically do. Perhaps this accounts, at least in part, for the empirical findings that suggest that parents who educate their children at home are doing a good job socializing them. In one study, Brian Ray of the National Home Education Research Institute surveyed over 7,300 adults who had been homeschooled, most for at least seven years. Ray found that homeschool graduates were significantly more involved in community and civic affairs, such as volunteering and working for political candidates, than were traditionally schooled adults. They also voted and attended public meetings at higher rates. Over 74% of the young adults surveyed had taken college classes compared to 46% of the traditionally schooled population. The overwhelming majority was gainfully employed or attending college. 98% of the homeschool graduates had read at least one book in the six months prior to the study, compared to 69% of the comparison group. Ray's study demonstrated that adult homeschoolers are happier and find life more exciting than their traditionally schooled peers. Other studies have concluded that homeschooled children are not socially isolated, that their self-concept, a barometer of socialization, tends to be better than traditionally schooled children, and that homeschooling fosters leadership skills at least as well as traditional schooling.

The British pediatrician and psychoanalyst D.W. Winnicott cautioned that there is a price to pay for education that neglects children's emotional and imaginative capacities. We can measure it, he said, "in terms of the loss of the opportunity for creative learning, as opposed to being taught." Creative learning is connected to Winnicott's concept of creative living, which he considers the foundation of health and happiness. He says, "In creative living you or I find that everything we do strengthens the feeling that we are alive, that we are ourselves." When children learn creatively, they retain a personal, self-directed sense of purpose that is unmistakably their own. And this can be measured in enthusiasm and vitality. The homeschoolers that I met are learning and living creatively.... Homeschooling represents a real alternative to traditional public education, as well as to the ideology of consumerism, conformity, and competition that permeates our increasingly standardized educational institutions.

Homeschooling Is a Widely Misunderstood Movement

Rachel Gathercole

Rachel Gathercole is a homeschooling advocate, teacher, speaker, and author whose book The Well-Adjusted Child: The Social Benefits of Homeschooling *was released in 2007.*

We're all familiar with the popular images of homeschoolers in America: Extreme fundamentalist families shutting out all other points of view. Tired mothers teaching in front of a blackboard after late nights of preparing lesson plans, or perhaps stumbling recklessly through unfamiliar subject matter they are not qualified to teach. Lonely, friendless children sitting at home, wistfully dreaming of an exciting, lively social life at school. Or worse, isolated little misfits tragically unaware that an outside world even exists.

These stereotypes are touted freely by the popular media and conventional schooling experts alike. We have probably all imagined them ourselves at one time or another. But they have little to do with the realities of homeschooling for most families today, and are rarely backed by factual data.

But even when we ignore these stereotypes and look to the news media for answers, it is hard to sort out what homeschooling is. The things we are told about it and the images portrayed are often contradictory and/or downright sensationalized. The mass media tell us on one hand that homeschoolers excel, and on the other hand that they are under-regulated. One minute we hear that it is hard for homeschoolers to get into college, and the next minute that they are going to Harvard. We are told that homeschooling is

Rachel Gathercole, "Homeschooling's True Colors: Examining the Myths and the Facts About America's Fastest-Growing Educational Movement," *Mothering*, July/August 2005, Reproduced by permission of the author.

difficult and requires an incredible degree of sacrifice by parents, yet the number of parents choosing to homeschool is skyrocketing.

Just what is the truth about homeschooling? The hard facts might surprise you.

Homeschooling Is Prevalent

Below are some common myths about homeschooling, and the simple facts behind this widely misunderstood movement.

Myth:

Homeschooling is a fringe movement, less prevalent than advocates suggest.

Fact:

The US Census Bureau reports that in 2001, more than 2 million children were being homeschooled in the US alone, and the number is rising at the astounding rate of 15 to 20 percent per year.[1]

Patricia M. Lines, the foremost homeschooling expert in the US Department of Education, further notes (in 1999) that since some families homeschool for only part of their children's school years, the number of children with some homeschooling experience, by age 18, would be around 6 to 12 percent of the population.[2] The percentage would be greater today.

Demographically speaking, the homeschooling population comprises families of all socioeconomic groups, religions, sizes, political affiliations, family structures, and ethnicities.[3–6] Statistically, homeschooling families tend to be large, conservative, white, two-parent families, and the average homeschooling parent has a moderate to high level of income and education.[7–10] However, according to the US Census Bureau, differences between homeschooling families and conventional-schooling families are not very large, and the demographic gap appears to be narrowing.[11]

Religion Is Only One Reason

Myth:

Homeschooling is a primarily religious phenomenon.

Fact:

According to the US Census Bureau and other sources, in 2000 only 33 percent of homeschooling parents cited religion as a reason for homeschooling (and many of these parents cited other reasons as well). On the other hand, 50.8 percent cited a belief that their children could get a better education through homeschooling, while 29.8 percent stated that school offers a poor learning environment, and 11.5 percent said that their children were not being challenged in school.[12]

According to the US Census Bureau ... only 33 percent of homeschooling parents cited religion as a reason for homeschooling.

Statistics that correctly state that the majority of home-schoolers in America identify themselves as Christian should not be mistaken for evidence that homeschooling is a religiously based phenomenon. The vast majority of Americans in general identify themselves as Christians—85 percent in 2003, according to a Gallup poll—so it is no surprise that the majority of both homeschoolers and conventional schoolers also identify themselves as Christian.[13–16] Some families choose homeschool, private school, or public school for religious reasons, and some homeschooling families are religious fundamentalists, just as some non-homeschooling families are. Like the general population, the homeschooling population comprises families of all religions, as well as many families who would classify themselves as agnostic, atheist, or unaffiliated with any established religion.[17]

Homeschoolers Excel Academically

Myth:

Homeschooled children are undereducated.

Fact:

Numerous studies of homeschoolers' achievement show that homeschoolers score exceptionally well on standardized tests, with the average/median homeschool students outperforming at least 70 to 80 percent of their conventionally schooled peers in all subjects and at all grade levels.[18,19] Studies also show that the longer a student is homeschooled, the higher his or her test scores become.[20] In addition, homeschoolers have been described as "dominating" national contests, such as the national spelling and geography bees, and are now sought by many colleges.[21–26]

Numerous studies of homeschoolers' achievement show that homeschoolers score exceptionally well on standardized tests.

Teaching Methods Vary

Myth:

Most homeschoolers learn through a formal curriculum, taught to them by their parents (for example, at the kitchen table).

Fact:

Homeschoolers learn through a variety of methods, which may include some teaching by the parent, as well as self-directed projects, real-life activities (such as gardening, cooking, sports, volunteer activities, etc.), free play, independent reading, group classes with other homeschoolers, cooperative learning experiences with other families, field trips and outings as a family or with a homeschooling group, and social activities and gatherings.[27–31] The majority of homeschooling families do not purchase prepackaged curriculums but instead use some individually created combination of the above methods determined by the parent and/or child to suit the child's individual needs and learning style.[32]

Homeschoolers also employ a wide range of overall approaches and philosophies, from "school-at-home" approaches that match the popular image, to (perhaps most common) an eclectic approach in which the family selects materials and activities according to the children's needs at the time, to unschooling—"delight-driven" or "child-led" learning in which the child learns all necessary material through pursuing his or her own interests in a real-world setting, with a parent available to help, answer questions, and direct the child to resources.[33–36] Those who engage in formal lessons do so to varying degrees: one family might purchase and adhere to a full curriculum, while another might devise a complete or partial curriculum of their own using alternative methods and focus; still another might reserve formal lessons for a particular subject area, such as math.[37–40]

As new and varied as these methods may sound, all are effective methods for home educating. Dr. Lawrence M. Rudner, in an independent study of more than 20,000 homeschoolers, found that though homeschoolers tend not to use prepackaged curriculum programs, they nevertheless score "exceptionally high" on standardized tests, ranking typically in the 70th to 80th percentile (compared to the national average of the 50th percentile). "It is readily apparent . . . that the median scores for home school students are well above their public/private school counterparts in every subject and in every grade," regardless of the presence or absence of formal curriculum use,[41] says Rudner. Homeschooled students, regardless of teaching method, have gone on to attend Ivy League universities. According to an article in *Stanford Magazine*, "among homeschoolers who end up at Stanford, 'self-teaching' is a common thread."[42,43]

The Socialization Issue

Myth:

Homeschoolers are "stuck at home."

Fact:

Per week, the average homeschooled child participates in at least five outside activities, such as sports teams, scouts, clubs, classes in the community, volunteer activities, etc.[44] Some (about 18 percent) participate in public school part-time.[45] Many homeschooling parents are also very involved in their communities—volunteering, attending or teaching classes, pursuing part-time or full-time careers, operating family businesses, and/or developing close friendships with other homeschooling families.[46,47] Homeschooling parents and children, free of externally imposed school schedules, are in charge of their time and are free to come and go as they please. Homeschooling enables family members to be very involved in outside activities without sacrificing their time together to do so.

Homeschooling enables family members to be very involved in outside activities without sacrificing their time together to do so.

Myth:

Homeschooling deprives children of proper socialization.

Fact:

Homeschooling affords children plenty of time and opportunity for social interaction and friendships, as well as time to learn appropriate social behaviors from their parents. The available research shows that homeschoolers tend to be very well adjusted. In 1986, even before the rapid growth in the homeschooling movement that we are seeing today, social researcher John Wesley Taylor V found that the self-concept of homeschooled children was significantly higher than that of their traditionally schooled peers when tested using the widely accepted Piers-Harris Children's Self-Concept Scale. Among his conclusions was the statement that "it would appear that few home-schooling children are socially deprived. Critics of the home school should not urge self-concept and socialization rationales. These factors apparently favor homeschoolers over the conventionally schooled population."[48]

More recently, psychotherapist Dr. Larry Shyers, in a study involving "blind" observation of the behavior of homeschooled and conventionally schooled children, found that home-schooled children exhibited significantly fewer "problem behaviors" than their conventionally sohooled peers and had no significant difference in levels of self-esteem.[49] Thomas Smedley, studying communication skills, socialization, and daily living skills through the Vineland Adaptive Behavior Scales, concluded that homeschooled kids in his study were more mature and better socialized than the conventionally schooled.[50] And finally, in a survey of adults who had been homeschooled for at least seven years, Dr. Brian D. Ray found that 59 percent said they were "very happy" with life, while only 27.6 percent of the general population said they were "very happy" with life.[51]

Homeschooled children exhibited significantly fewer "problem behaviors" . . . and had no significant difference in level of self-esteem.

Due to the excellent teacher-student ratio that homeschoolers enjoy and the lack of time-consuming administrative tasks such as attendance taking, busywork, etc., the academic aspects of homeschooling require only a fraction of the time necessary for the same tasks in a conventional school setting, leaving lots of extra time for social activities. Not limited by strict "school hours" and brief interactions in the hall, homeschooled children are often found instead spending long days at the park with friends, gathering with other kids for group activities, sleeping over at each other's houses on week-nights or weekends, and enjoying long conversations with their parents and siblings.[52,53] Homeschooled children also tend to have both homeschooled and conventionally schooled friends, and, like conventionally schooled children, they can and do play with neighborhood children and participate in scouts, 4H, church groups, community bands, orchestras, and sports groups, as well as outside classes such as dance and martial arts.[54-56] Many homeschooling parents consider their children's social learning to be as integral a part of their education as academic subjects, and they are careful to provide their children with both social skills and opportunities to use them.

Myth:

Homeschoolers are insulated from the real world, democracy, and diversity.

Fact:

Homeschooling families live and learn in the real world (see methods outlined above), typically interacting with real people of various ages and backgrounds on a real-world basis rather than just with peers in a classroom. They have time and proximity to observe firsthand the social and political activities of their parents, who, according to Patricia M. Lines's report in the *ERIC Digest*, "are more likely to vote, contribute money to political causes, contact elected officials about their views, attend public meetings or rallies, or join community and volunteer associations" than are the parents of conventionally schooled children.[57] "This holds true even when researchers compare only families with similar characteristics, including education, age, race, family structure, geographic region, and number of hours worked per week."[58] Moreover, homeschoolers are a diverse population (see above) and often have lots of freedom to travel to diverse locations for both educational and social purposes.

Achievement Is an Outcome

Myth:

Homeschoolers have a hard time applying for, getting into, and adjusting to college.

Fact:

College admissions officers now seek out homeschoolers due to their excellent preparation for academic success at college. An article in *Stanford Magazine* indicates that Stanford has a "special interest" in homeschoolers, and is "eager to embrace them" despite their lack of formal credentials. "The distinguishing factor is intellectual vitality," says Dr. Jonathan Reider, a former senior associate director of undergraduate admissions at Stanford and a national expert on college-bound homeschoolers. "These kids have it, and everything they do is responding to it."[59] David and Micki Colfax, authors of the well-known book *Homeschooling for Excellence*, homeschooled four sons, three of whom attended Harvard.[60] These are just a few examples; Karl M. Bundaya's well-known website (www.learninfreedom.org) lists more than 1,000 colleges and universities, including Ivy League schools and many other very selective and prestigious schools, that have readily admitted homeschoolers.[61]

Myth:

Parents without teaching certificates, college degrees, and so on are not qualified to teach their children.

Fact:

Rudner's large study (mentioned earlier) found that there is "no significant difference" in homeschoolers' achievement according to whether or not a parent is certified to teach. "For those who would argue that only certified teachers should be allowed to teach their children at home, these findings suggest that such a requirement would not meaningfully affect student achievement."[62] Another study, by Dr. Brian Ray, similarly found that while homeschooled students scored on average in the 76th percentile or higher in reading, language, and math, children of certified teachers had no advantage over children whose parents were not certified teachers.[63]

The Issue of Regulation

Myth:

Greater government regulation is needed to make homeschooling a more viable or valid option.

Fact:

There is plenty of evidence that increased regulation is unnecessary for homeschoolers. In addition to the studies cited above showing that teacher certification and use of a formal curriculum are not relevant factors in homeschoolers' achievement, a study of more than 5,000 students from 1,657 families found that homeschoolers score very high on standardized tests, even when their state does not highly regulate.[64]

Keeping in mind that the average homeschooled student appears to exceed the achievement of her or his average conventionally schooled peer, it is illogical to impose curriculum or other requirements aimed at making homeschooling more school-like or requiring homeschools to adhere to the standards of public or conventional schools. Such regulations would be superfluous and could potentially lower the level of achievement by removing the freedom and flexibility that make homeschooling so effective.

Myth:

Homeschooling is associated with neglect and abuse.

Fact:

There is no evidence that homeschoolers are at higher risk for neglect or abuse than publicly or privately schooled children.[65] In fact, there is reason to believe that neglect and abuse are actually less common in homeschool situations.[66,67] Moreover, 85 percent of child fatalities occur in children younger than six years of age, before children begin their formal schooling in any form.[68]

Effect on Public Schools

Myth:

Homeschooling is a threat to the public schools. Homeschoolers abandon or "suck the life out of" public schools in their choice to homeschool.

Fact:

Homeschoolers and public schools are, in many ways, boons to one another. By removing their children from public schools, homeschoolers inadvertently help the schools by relieving overcrowding and freeing up resources for other students while still paying the taxes that fund public education. In this way, homeschoolers actually save taxpayers millions of dollars per year.[69] To put it another way, every child who is homeschooled opens up a free seat in a classroom for another child. In this sense, every time 3 to 10 new taxpaying families (or about 20 new homeschooled kids) choose to homeschool, it is as if a new teacher has been hired for the public schools at no cost to taxpayers. Thus the growth of homeschooling is the equivalent of a host of new, high-achieving schools being built to relieve overcrowding and reduce class size at no expense to taxpayers.

Moreover, it is private schools, not public schools, that appear to bear the true brunt of reduced enrollment. While enrollment in public schools and home schools continues to grow with the population, enrollment in private schools remains stagnant.[70] In other words, it appears statistically that the majority of homeschooling parents would otherwise be sending their children to private school, not public school. Finally, it has been noted that educators in conventional schooling situations stand to learn much from homeschoolers, who are conducting field research on education that can never be conducted in a school setting, even as they educate their kids very successfully. As the late educator John Holt commented: "It is a research project done at no cost, of a kind for which neither the public schools nor the government could afford to pay."[71] He also wrote: "From these people and their work, all serious schools and teachers, many of them now severely limited and handicapped by the conditions under which they have to work, stand to learn a great deal."[72]

Whatever images pass through the media and popular culture, the facts of homeschooling ultimately speak for themselves. As more and more homeschoolers grow up and become adult citizens, perceptions of homeschoolers will gradually change, but the facts will remain the same. Although it is understandable that perceptions and fears exist, there is a reason that homeschooling is growing at the rate it is. There is a reason that so many educated parents are choosing it despite popular stereotypes and assumptions. The reason is simple: In the face of fact, those muddled images are cleanly washed away by homeschooling's true colors.

Flying colors.

Homeschooling's True Colors: Notes

Issue 131

1. Kurt J. Bauman, "Home Schooling in the United States: Trends and Characteristics," Working Paper Series 51 (Washington, DC: US Census Bureau Population Division, 2001): 2.

2. Patricia M. Lines, "Homeschoolers: Estimating Numbers and Growth," National Institute on Student Achievement, Curriculum, and Assessment, Office of Educational Research and Improvement, US Department of Education, Web Edition (Spring 1999; previously released as a paper in Spring 1998): www.ed.gov/offices/OERI/SAI/homeschool/index.html

3. Personal interviews.

4. Lawrence M. Rudner, "Scholastic Achievement and Demographic Characteristics of Home School Students in

1998," HSLDA (1999): www.hslda.org/docs/study/ rudner1999/FullText.asp www.hslda.org/docs/study/ rudner1999/Rudner2.asp www.hslda.org/docs/study/ rudner1999/Rudner2.asp

5. Stacey Bielick et al., "Homeschooling in the United States: 1999," NCES Technical Report (Washington, DC: US Department of Education, National Center for Education Statistics, 2001): 2001–2033; http://nces.ed .gov/programs/quarterly/vol_3/3_3/q3-2.asp

6. See Note 1: 6–13

7. See Note 5.

8. Robin R. Henke et al., "Issues Related to Estimating the Home Schooled Population in the United States," NCES Technical Report (Washington, DC: US Department of Education, National Center for Education Statistics, 2000): 2001–2311; http://nces.ed.gov/pubsearch/ pubsinfo.asp?pubid=2000311

9. See Note 4.

10. See Note 6.

11. See Note 1: 10.

12. See Note 1: 8–13.

13. Lydia Saad, "Religion Is Very Important to Majority of Americans," Gallup News Service, World Wide Religious News (5 December 2003): http://209.157.64.200/ focus/f-news/1034289/posts

14. Egon Mayer et al., "American Religious Identification Survey" (New York: Graduate Center of the City University of New York, 2001): www.gc.cuny.edu/studies/ aris_index.htm

15. "Religious Beliefs of Americans" (2004): www .religioustolerance.org/chr_poll3.htm

16. "Beliefs: General Religious" (2005): www.barna.org/ FlexPage.aspx?Page=Topic&TopicID=2

17. Patricia M. Lines, "Homeschooling," ERIC Digest (Oregon: Clearinghouse on Educational Management, College of Education, University of Oregon, September 2001): 2.

18. See Note 4.

19. Brian D. Ray, Home Schooling on the Threshold: A Survey of Research at the Dawn of the New Millennium (Salem, OR: National Home Education Research Institute, 1999).

20. Brian D. Ray, Strengths of their Own: Home Schoolers Across America (Salem, OR: NHERI, 1997).

21. Vaishali Honawar, "National 'Bees' Buzz with Home Schoolers," The Washington Times (21 May 2002).

22. Dean Reynolds, "Home Schoolers Strong Competitors in Spelling Bee," www.abcnews.com (29 May 2003): 1–2.

23. Rich Jefferson, "Home Schoolers Win First, Second, and Third at National Spelling Bee" (2001): 1–2; www.hslda.org/docs/news/hslda/200006010.asp

24. Jennifer Vernon, "Washington State Eighth Grader Wins National Geographic Bee," National Geographic News (21 May 2003): 1–4.

25. Jennifer Vernon, "Ten Students Advance to Geographic Bee Finals," National Geographic News (20 May 2003): 1–6.

26. Stentor Danielson, "Geographic Bee Champ: Michigan Ten-Year-Old," National Geographic News (22 May 2002): 1–5.

27. See Note 3.

28. Christine Foster, "In a Class by Themselves,"Stanford Magazine (November/December 2000): 1–11.

29. Grace Llewellyn, The Teenage Liberation Handbook: How to Quit School and Get a Real Life and Education (Eugene, OR: Lowry House Publishers, 1998).

30. David Guterson, Family Matters: Why Homeschooling Makes Sense (New York: Harcourt, Brace, Jovanovich, 1992): 11–36.

31. David and Micki Colfax, Homeschooling for Excellence (New York: Warner Books, 1988).

32. See Note 4.

33. See Note 29.

34. John Holt, Teach Your Own: A Hopeful Path for Education (New York: Bantam/Doubleday/Dell, 1981): 125–146, 208–232.

35. See Note 28: 7.

36. See Note 3.

37. See Note 29.

38. See Note 34.

39. See Note 28: 7.

40. See Note 3.

41. See Note 4.

42. See Note 31.

43. See Note 28: 7.

44. See Note 19.

45. See Note 5.

46. See Note 3.

47. See Note 17: 3.

48. John Wesley Taylor V, Self Concept in Home-Schooling Children, doctoral dissertation (Michigan: Andrews University, 1986); summarized in Home School Researcher 2, no. 2 (1986): 2–8.

49. Larry E. Shyers, Comparison of Social Adjustment Between Home and Traditionally Schooled Students, doctoral dissertation (Gainesville: University of Florida, 1992): 306–311.

50. Thomas C. Smedley, "The Socialization of Homeschool Children," master's thesis (Radford, VA: Radford University, 1992); summarized in Home School Researcher 8, no. 3 (1992): 9–16.

51. See Note 19.

52. See Note 3.

53. See Note 29: 138–149.

54. See Note 3.

55. See Note 19.

56. See Note 5.

57. See Note 17.

58. See Note 17.

59. See Note 28: 2–11.

60. See Note 31.

61. Karl M. Bunday, Learn in Freedom! (2000): http://learninfreedom.org/colleges_4_hmsc.html

62. See Note 4

63. See Note 19.

64. See Note 20.

65. National Home Education Network, "Thoughts on Protecting Children in Homeschooling Families: The NHEN Response to Questions Posed by the North Carolina Task Force of Child Fatalities" (2002): www.nhen.org/LegInfo/default.asp?id=420

66. National Clearinghouse on Child Abuse and Neglect Information, "Child Maltreatment 2001: Summary of Key Findings" (2001): http://nrcys.ou.edu/pdfs/publications/cmsummary.pdf and http://nccanch.acf.hhs.gov/pubs/factsheets/canstats.pdf

67. J. Michael Smith, "CBS Scare Stories Miss the Mark Badly"The Washington Times (3 November 2003).

Posted as "The Dark Side of CBS"at www.hslda.org/docs/news/washingtontimes/200311040.asp

68. See Note 66.

69. Ray, Brian D. National Home Education Research Institute, "Facts on Homeschooling" (8 January 2003): www.nheri.org/modules.php?name=Content&pa=show page&pid=21, 1.

70. Patricia M. Lines, "Homeschooling Comes of Age," The Public Interest, Discovery Institute (1 July 2000): 2, www.discovery.org/scripts/viewDB/index.php?program =Misc&command=view&id=277

71. John Holt, "Schools and Homeschoolers: A Fruitful Partnership," Phi Delta Kappan (February 1983): 393.

72. See Note 34: 330–331.

Homeschoolers Are Excelling

Andrea Neal

Andrea Neal is an eighth-grade English and history teacher at St. Richard's School in Indianapolis, Indiana, and an adjunct scholar with the Indiana Policy Review, a nonprofit education foundation focused on state and municipal issues.

Excelling in and out of the home, home-schooled kids are thriving across the country. Students demonstrating exceptional academic honors are capturing the top slots at national competitions.

Recognized for Achievement

It wasn't so long ago that home-schoolers like Johanna Schilling, Jonathan Gainer and Eli Owens were oddballs in the education landscape. Not anymore.

You name the contest—National Spelling Bee, National Geographic Bee, National Merit Scholarship—and chances are good that home-school kids have participated, performed with distinction, and won. These days, headlines of academic achievement are as likely to feature home-schooled children as their peers from traditional public and private school settings. Perhaps just as noteworthy, nobody's jaw drops when it happens.

[In 2006], four home-schooled students were named semifinalists in the Presidential Scholars competition, which recognizes the nation's most distinguished high-school graduates. The honor served notice of two important trends: one, home-schoolers have entered the mainstream of academic achievement; two, they're being recognized for it.

Home-Schoolers Win Prestigious Awards

Stories abound of home-schoolers' success:

At 17, Johanna was recognized as the first home-school winner of a $40,000 Ruth DeYoung Kohler Scholarship for Artistic Merit in her home state of Wisconsin. She will use the money to pursue her studies at the Houghton College school of music in New York.

It's not surprising that a home-schooler gets much better academic results. There's just no way around the structure.

Eli, 19, a home-school graduate who attends West Virginia University, was named a 2006–2007 Goldwater Scholar. He was one of 323 college students nationally to receive the award, established by Congress to encourage advanced studies by select sophomores and juniors who excel in math, science and engineering.

Jonathan, 14, was the first home-schooler picked for the Kelley Junior Executive Institute, a summer program at Indiana University that identifies 50 high-achieving, primarily minority high-school students interested in studying business. Note that he's the age of a typical eighth grader, yet he's already completed Algebra II.

These stories are just the tip of the iceberg. In 2005, a home-schooler won the National Geographic Bee. Home-schoolers swept the first three spots in the 2000 National Spelling Bee. In 2003, the latest year for which figures are available, a record 129 home-schoolers were named National Merit Scholars, an increase of more than 600 percent over 1995. The estimated 1.8 million home-schoolers—out of 54 million children in kindergarten through high school—seem to be achieving honors disproportionate to their numbers.

Structure Makes a Difference

"It's not surprising that a home-schooler gets much better academic results. There's just no way around the structure," says Ian Slatter, director of media relations for the Home School Legal Defense Association in Virginia.

Yes, structure matters. Although it varies by family, the typical home-school consists of one parent teaching one or more children in the home. But not just in the home. Home-schoolers take field trips and visit museums and libraries. They network with other home-school families. They use books and curricula that reflect their own academic and religious values, yet align closely enough to state academic standards that students are prepared for standardized tests, which some states require. In a home-school, the teacher-student ratio for any given lesson is 1:1 or 1:2. Not even an elite private school, where class size is capped at 6 or 18, can rival that.

The structure works especially well in the elementary years as students are mastering math and reading skills that will be the foundation for later learning. When course work grows more complex, many home-school families contract with experts to teach their children more advanced subjects, sometimes pooling resources to create small classrooms not too different from a traditional school.

Because of structure and flexibility, the typical home-school student can complete graduation requirements by age 16.

Flexibility Is Key to Success

It's the flexibility that so many home-schooling families lift up as the key ingredient. In home-school, parents can quickly identify a student's areas of strength and weakness, offering enrichment opportunities for the former and focused attention on the latter.

Those with a gift for music can take instrument lessons or catch a symphony matinee when their traditional classmates are in school. Johanna, for example, spent up to three hours a day practicing piano for 10 years. Computer whizzes can seek out apprenticeships with nearby businesses; those who love sports can finish their workout in the morning before the YMCA gets crowded.

Because of structure and flexibility, the typical home-school student can complete graduation requirements by age 16. As a result, some go to college early; many enroll in local community colleges until their parents deem them ready to live on a campus with older students. . . .

Growth of Home-Schooling as an Option

Although evangelical Christians remain the single biggest group in the home-schooling movement, they are by no means the only ones. In her book *Homeschoolers' Success Stories*, Linda Dobson notes that "families from every conceivable religious, economic, political, and philosophical background in the United States" have realized the benefits to home-schooling.

"This wave has been impelled by home-schooling's greater visibility as an educational option; local, state, and national home-schooling support groups; easy networking and information sharing via the Internet and e-mail; and continuing government-school problems, such as dumbed-down curriculum, violence, drugs, bullying, and more," she writes. . . .

What has changed is public understanding and acceptance of the home-school phenomenon. The percentage of those feeling that home-schooling is a "bad thing" dropped from 73 percent in 1985 to 57 percent in 1997, according to a Phi Delta Kappa (PDK)/Gallup poll. In a 1999 poll, PDK asked if public schools should make services available to children who are schooled at home, and a surprising number of respondents said yes. The numbers ranged from a high of 92 percent for special education courses for disabled or handicapped children to a low of 53 percent for transportation services.

There are critics, to be sure, including members of the National Education Association, the powerful teachers' union. . . .

Data Supports Home-Schoolers

The data, however, are on the home-schoolers' side.

In the most significant study to date, "Scholastic Achievement and Demographic Characteristics of Home School Students in 1998," researcher Lawrence M. Rudner made the following findings:

- Almost 25 percent of home-school students are enrolled one or more grades above their age-level peers in public and private schools.

- Home-school student achievement test scores are exceptionally high. The median scores for every subtest at every grade (typically in the 70th to 80th percentile) are well above those of public and Catholic/private school students.

- On average, home-school students in grades one to four perform one grade level above their age-level public or private school peers on achievement tests.

- The achievement test score gap between home-school students and public or private school students starts to widen in grade five.

- Students who have been home-schooled their entire academic life have higher scholastic-achievement test scores than students who have also attended other educational programs.

Smaller studies have affirmed the findings, and Slatter says his organization hopes to do an updated achievement study in the near future. . . .

Yes, home-schools have entered the mainstream of America's educational system, and their students intend to compete with the best and brightest in the country.

Homeschooling Is Not for Everyone

Carole Moore

Carole Moore is a former law enforcement officer and writer based in Jacksonville, North Carolina.

I became interested in homeschooling a few years ago when a friend told me how much she loved it. A former cop turned writer, I approached the editor at the newspaper where I worked and convinced him to let me write a series on the topic. I interviewed dozens of homeschooling parents and students. All told, including the work on the series plus my own follow-up research, I spent over a year studying the possibility and debating whether learning at home would be best for my kids—a daughter, then age 10, and a son, age 8.

I learned that many families homeschooled because they didn't like the secular curriculum. Others complained that classes were dumbed down, which caused boredom and restlessness in bright students. A lot chose to remove their kids from what they perceived as an unhealthy social atmosphere. All were convinced they'd done the right thing.

They explained the differences in the types of homeschooling to me: Some followed rigorous religious-based curricula, while others used the same materials as their public schools. A few, called unschoolers, followed nothing but their hearts and let the kids themselves pick what they wanted to study. Many bartered with other parents on subjects requiring special expertise, such as trading French instruction for piano lessons.

The kids' education seemed balanced and academically sound, but most appealing was the bond they shared with their parents. My own daughter, anxious to grow up, nibbled at her ties to me, with her younger brother fast on her heels. I wondered if homeschooling could bring us closer.

Some of the most troubled kids I dealt with came from homes where they'd been very sheltered.

Still, as I spoke with homeschooling families from one coast to the other, certain troubling questions bubbled to the surface—many of them familiar to me from my days in law enforcement.

Our community is nowhere near a major city. Still my children went to elementary school with a girl whose father committed suicide in her presence, kids with both parents in prison, and youngsters who couldn't read, yet knew all the words to filthy rap songs. As a police officer, I often dealt with adolescent drug dealers, pregnant teens, and runaways—kids whose lives were out of control. Certainly the largest majority of them were enrolled in public schools, but not all. Some of the most troubled kids I dealt with came from homes where they'd been very sheltered.

I remember one teenager in particular. After years of alternately being homeschooled and attending a very strict, small, church-based school, she moved to a public school—where she spiraled out of control. She drank. She took drugs. And she had sex. Her parents were appalled; that was not how they'd raised their daughter.

Some would blame the influence of the public school system. They'd say she made friends with bad kids. And they'd be right. But that wasn't the only reason she got into so much trouble. In my opinion, her problem went much deeper: she didn't know how to handle the sudden combination of freedom and exposure to a side of life she'd never personally confronted. Her parents had talked about these things. She'd heard about them in church. But talk alone isn't a substitute for reality, and the forbidden often looms sweet and tantalizing by virtue of its mystery.

Academics form only part of the equation when it comes to teaching life skills. Kids need to know how to write a persuasive essay, but they also should learn about real life and, in the process, develop the skills they need to cope with it.

We can't raise our children in carefully controlled environments and expect them to instinctively know how to handle evil.

My daughter, who now attends a public high school, has made good choices in both her academic and social lives so far. We've talked about sex, but nothing I've ever said to her has provided as strong a deterrent to casual, early sex as the girl in her class with the ever-expanding belly. Nothing makes my daughter more aware of the effects of drugs than seeing burnt-out kids. And nothing brings home the consequences of drinking and driving than the empty seat of a boy who did just that.

They're tough lessons, but ones she will never forget. Seeing the aftermath of negative behavior with her own eyes impresses her much more than simple words or even our own good examples.

Do I like that my children are exposed to life's underbelly? Of course not. I'd much prefer to bring them up in an atmosphere of innocence and trust. But we can't raise our children in carefully controlled environments and expect them to instinctively know how to handle evil. Pretending that it doesn't exist won't make it go away.

Homeschooling would have built a wall around my kids and kept them safe—for a little while. Ultimately, they would have had to go out into the real world. Public school has exposed them to bad influences as well as good ones. I believe they're stronger for having had to make tough choices. And going through it together has strengthened our relationship, making it easier for me to start letting go of their hands.

Should Homeschooling Be Regulated?

Chapter Preface

In February 2008, a California appellate court ruled that parents in that state must have a teaching credential to homeschool their children. After declaring that homeschooling was not a constitutional right, the judge went on to warn that instructors teaching without credentials would be subject to criminal action. Uncredentialed parents who did not provide a credentialed tutor or send their children to a public or private school that requires daily attendance could be prosecuted for truancy, as well as lose custody. The ruling, one of the most controversial in recent years, made most homeschooling in the state illegal and shocked and angered the homeschooling community nationwide. Many supporters of homeschooling viewed the ruling as an outright attack on the very idea of homeschooling.

At the time of the ruling, California was considered a state with low regulation for homeschooling. It offered four legal homeschooling options: (1) qualifying as a private school, (2) using a private tutor, (3) enrolling in a private school satellite program, or (4) enrolling in an independent study program offered through a public school. Only those parents who declared their homeschooling program a private school had to provide official notice to the state, and only those parents who chose to teach as a private tutor had to be certified.

The California episode is just one of a number over the years in the ongoing battle over whether homeschools should be subject to government legislation or regulation. Some homeschooling parents are not totally opposed to a small or moderate degree of oversight. Others believe it is their fundamental right to decide what is best for their children and are opposed to any and all homeschooling legislation or regulation. They resist any involvement at the federal, state, or local level and view legislative and regulatory actions as a means for anti-homeschooling supporters to weaken homeschooling or get rid of it entirely.

The National Education Association (NEA), on the other hand, sanctions the idea that parents who teach their own children should be licensed by the state, use a state-approved curriculum, and pay all their own expenses. While not all opponents of homeschooling agree in full with the NEA, most believe strongly that some regulation is necessary to ensure accountability and that homeschooled children should master certain levels before they "graduate."

The issue is a complex one. The general requirements regarding education are laid out at the federal level. But for the most part, the responsibility for public education falls to state and local government, and no two states treat homeschooling in exactly the same way. Homeschooling regulation is a result of compulsory school attendance laws, which vary from state to state. As a result, even though currently about two-thirds of all states have specific laws authorizing and regulating homeschooling, each has different homeschooling regulations. According to the Home School Legal Defense Association (HSLDA), there are four categories of legal options for homeschooling: states requiring no notice, states with low regulation, states with moderate regulation, and states with high regulation.

In the ten states that have no requirements for homeschooling, parents do not even have to notify the state that they are homeschooling their children. This is not to say that these states all have the same regulations beyond no notice. Texas, for example, is a no-notice state. In Texas, a homeschooling family must establish and operate its homeschool as a private school, and the parents must teach grammar, reading, spelling, good citizenship, and math. Indiana is another no-notice state. Indiana does not have any requirements for curricula or formats for math, science, or social studies. It does have a statute that requires home educators to provide an equal program of learning, but there is no enforcement.

In the fourteen states with low regulation, all that parents have to do is notify the state that they are homeschooling their children. In the fifteen states with moderate regulation, parents not only must notify the state of their intent to home-school but also must submit test scores and/or professional evaluation of their children's academic progress. In the eleven states with high regulation, in addition to notifying the state that they are homeschooling their children, parents must submit achievement test scores and/or professional evaluations and fulfill other requirements such as use of state-approved curricula or teacher-certification of parents. In some cases, they must permit home visits by state officials.

States Must Maintain Control and Oversight of Education

Louis A. Greenfield

Louis A. Greenfield is an attorney currently practicing law in New York and New Jersey.

Home-schooling and religious beliefs are a familiar combination. While religious beliefs are not the only reason for home-schooling, it appears that religion plays a significant role in home-schooling programs. At the very least, the topic of home-schooling for religious reasons receives a lot of attention. A primary focus for home-schooled children is religious values. Parents of home-schooled children more and more are challenging the monitoring of their programs by the government, claiming that their religious values are being compromised. . . .

Resisting Government Intrusion

This debate regarding what regulations over home-schooling should be in place, if any, has viewpoints located at two completely opposite ends of the spectrum. At one end, there are those who view education as a compelling interest of the state; perhaps its most compelling interest and primary function. Those with this view would most likely favor more government regulation of home-schooling. On the other end of the spectrum are those who see education as inherently religious in nature. This end of the spectrum would likely, in part, consist of those who home-school their children for religious purposes and object to government monitoring of their home-schooling programs. . . .

As home-schooling became accepted by the courts as a legitimate means of education, home-schooling parents shifted

Louis A. Greenfield, "Religious Home-Schools: That's Not A Monkey On Your Back, It's a Compelling State Interest," *Rutgers Journal of Law and Religion*, vol. 9, Fall 2007, pp. 1–28. Reproduced by permission.

their attention to challenging regulations that monitor these home-schooling programs. Some were successful and some were not. While it is evident that many of these home-schooling parents want the government completely out of the education of their children, I believe that they will most likely not get their way since the state has a duty to enforce a compelling interest in ensuring their citizens are adequately educated. . . .

Some parents believe that it is a God-given right to home-school their children.

It appears that religious reasons [for home-schooling] provoke higher standards of scrutiny. While this trend tends to make the restrictions for religious home-schools more lax than non-secular home-schools, religious home-schools will still be exposed to some regulation and monitoring due to the state's compelling interest in the education of its citizens. These methods of monitoring include standardized testing, teacher certification requirements, and the submission of portfolios used to monitor the progress of the home-schooled children. . . .

Religious Motivation

According to a 1999 survey that asked why parents home-school their children, the top three reasons provided were the following: (1) a better education could be offered at home, (2) religious reasons, and (3) there was a poor learning environment at public school. While, according to this study, the leading reason why parents home-school their children is because the parents believe that they can do a better job than the public system, and often do, a more controversial discussion (and one more relevant to this paper) arises when one explores the religious reasons why children are home-schooled and the issues that arise from such home-schooling programs.

Some parents believe that it is a God-given right to home-school their children. These families tend to live and die by the word of the Bible and try to use this theory as a means of casting out state monitoring from their home-school program. At most, this theory can show that one's religious beliefs are genuine; on its own, it cannot stymie government monitoring. . . .

More extreme religious reasons also motivate parents to home-school their children. Christian Fundamentalists tend to use these more extreme religious reasons for home-schooling. "The main reason these Fundamentalist Christian parents opt out of public schools is their perception that [according to Neal Devins in the 1992 *George Washington Law Review*] the 'secularization of public schools . . . denies their right to oversee the upbringing of their children as they see fit.'" . . . These fundamentalists are, by and large, those who are objecting to state monitoring home-schooling programs. . . .

A parent merely has to receive church backing to begin instruction with little interference from the state.

Regulation Varies by State

So, what reasons do the states provide to justify the monitoring of home educational programs? [As Eric A. DeGroff writes in the 2003 *BYU Journal of Education and Law*,] "States have a substantial interest in ensuring that all children receive an adequate education." As a result of this substantial interest, the states must ensure that [as De Groff writes,] "schools perform their basic educational function and . . . meet certain minimum standards." In the private school context, the state justifies their mandated approval or accreditation to [De Groff continues,] "ensure compliance with its educational standards."

Religious vs. Secular Home-Schooling

In a study on education statutes in Alabama, the regulation of home-schooling in the United States is categorized into a number of distinct approaches. One of these approaches [comments William L. Campbell Jr. in the Winter 2001 *Alabama Law Review*,] "involves states enacting statutes that expressly allow for home-schooling but also provide for some form of state approval or notification by the parents to the local school board." The strictest of these approaches requires home-school teacher certification and permission from the state to home-school. . . .

The question of which approach is used depends on the type of home-schooling program. If the home-schooling program is a "church school," it will receive a more lenient degree of state regulation than if the program is not backed by a church. As a result of this dichotomy, a parent merely has to receive church backing to begin instruction with little interference from the state.

One of the most hotly contested methods of state monitoring of non-public schools programs (including home-school programs) are teacher certification requirements.

However, while the specific challenges to home-schooling statutes often vary depending on whether or not the home-schooling program is religious based, their respective outcomes may turn out to be the same. . . .

Certification Requirements

One of the most hotly contested methods of state monitoring of non-public schools programs (including home-school programs) are teacher certification requirements. Religious schools, almost always oppose mandatory certification for a variety of reasons. In order for a court to allow any sort of teaching certification requirement, the government must show that such a requirement [according to Campbell] "is rationally related to a legitimate state interest."

Statutes mandating teacher certification are not illegal, per se. While the teacher certification statutes have been overturned in some states, mainly because they were viewed as unreasonable, other state and federal courts have found such a requirement reasonable. Although teacher certification requirements are not illegal, per se, there is a strong objection to them. . . .

Courts have treated the enforcement of teaching certification requirements for home-school instructors differently, depending on whether the home-school was backed by a church (religious reasons) or was non-religious based. For example, in Alabama, all teachers are required to receive state certification except those teaching at church schools. This difference in teaching certification requirements indicates a disparate treatment of home-schooling programs. . . .

A home-school monitoring program should, at bare-minimum, require . . . each home-schooled child to take an annual standardized achievement test.

Teacher Certification Necessary

I believe that a teacher certification requirement should be necessary regardless of the reason for home-schooling. However, the acquisition of such a certification should require a minimum burden on the parents. Therefore, the educator should have, at minimum, a high school education (or an equivalent) and the parent's proficiency of this level should be proven by a standardized test. I also believe that each home-schooling parent must be made aware of any standards that their children would be required to meet, including test scores, subjects they would be required to teach, and hours of study. The parents awareness should be memorialized by a signed form.

Perhaps the most common method of state monitoring is achieved through standardized testing requirements. Typically, home-schooled children are required to take a standardized achievement test annually as a means of measuring their progress. The reason this method of monitoring is so common may be due to its lack of intrusiveness on both the home-schooled child and the family. . . .

A home-school monitoring program should, at bare-minimum, require . . . each home-schooled child to take an annual standardized achievement test. . . .

Mandated Monitoring Program

This country places the freedom of religion as one of the most important values. We see this freedom everywhere in our society, from special tax treatment for religious groups to religious garb in public. However, this freedom is not unlimited. As has been shown, there is an ongoing struggle between home-schooling parents (both secular and non-secular) and the government as to how much regulation and monitoring of home-schooling programs should be allowed.

There are many religious-based home-schooling parents that would like nothing better than to be left completely alone in the education of their children. However, this will not happen. The government has a compelling interest in the education of their citizens and must ensure that this education takes place using the least restrictive means available. This least restrictive requirement sets the government's limitation on home-school regulation. With these parameters in mind, the state should mandate a home-schooling monitoring program for religious and non-religious based programs as follows. Note that I group both religious and non-religious based programs together because these requirements will not restrict what can be taught or practiced at home. These requirements will ensure minimum standards for home-schooling programs in the least burdensome way. While I do not necessarily agree with this disparate treatment, it is the prevailing law and I will work within its parameters.

First and foremost, each home-schooled child should be required to take a monitored annual standardized achievement test. The Arkansas home-schooling statute provides an excellent example on how this requirement should be administered. A parent gets to choose the exact test to be administered from a pre-approved list. If a child does not meet the minimum scores for their age level, they must be placed into a public, private, or parochial school.

Essential Monitoring Components

Second, and probably most controversial, there should be a certification requirement for home-schooling teachers. Many states require that a parent hold at least a GED [General Education Development certificate], as they should. In addition to this GED requirement, I propose that home-schooling teachers be required to take a standardized test similar to the Praxis 1 exam that substitute teachers in New Jersey are required to pass. No extra classes and no exorbitant degrees; just pass a test. Anyone with a high school education should be qualified to pass such an exam. Due to the minimum knowledge requirement, this would place a small, but necessary, burden on home-schooling parents in order to ensure their qualifications.

Finally, each home-schooled child should be required to submit a portfolio at the beginning and middle of each academic year based on a state pre-approved list of the minimum educational requirements for a child of that age. The list would be available to every home-schooling parent before submitting the portfolio. The first portfolio should show what the parent intends to teach the child for the first half of the year. The second portfolio should include samples of the child's work showing what he or she has accomplished during the first half of the year and what the parent plans to teach during the second half of the year. The child's work in the second portfolio will serve as evidence that the child is being taught what was outlined in the first portfolio. Each portfolio would need to be approved by administrators and its approval would be based on whether it meets the list of pre-approved requirements. No portfolio would be needed at the end of the academic year due to the standardized achievement test.

Educational Welfare Must Be Monitored

Meg Jalsevac

Meg Jalsevac writes for LifeSiteNews.com, a nonprofit Internet service dedicated to issues of culture, life, and family.

Honorable Thomas Zampino of the Family Division of the New Jersey Superior Court has penalized a home-schooling mother of seven. According to a report by Matt Bowman on the website constitutionallycorrect.com, the mother's supposed infraction is home-schooling her children without supervision from the local school board—a right explicitly upheld in New Jersey law.

According to the court's opinion, Tara Hamilton is the defendant in a suit brought against her by her recently estranged husband, Stephen Hamilton. Stephen brought the suit in an attempt to force Tara to enroll their school-age children, aged 12 to 4 years, in parochial school because he believes that they are not receiving an adequate education while being home-schooled. All seven children currently reside with Tara.

Not in Children's Best Interest

According to the court document, Stephen claims that "continued home schooling is not in the children's best interest, they lack socialization skills and that it is too difficult for the mother to teach the children at five different grade levels. The father argues that the children are not receiving an education equivalent to a public or parochial school."

Prior to the marital discord that led to this suit, the Hamiltons had similarly home-schooled all of their school-age children.

Meg Jalsevac, "New Jersey Judge Scolds Mom for Home-Schooling, Throws Judicial Temper Tantrum," *LifeSiteNews.com*, March 7, 2007. Reproduced by permission.

In an effort to implement "certain basic requirements and safeguards," the Judge ordered Tara to submit her home-schooling children to standardized tests supplied by the local school district despite NJ law which says, "A child educated elsewhere than at school is not required to sit for a state or district standardized test."

The judge also ordered the local school board to file a suit against Tara in order to be able to "evaluate the instruction in the home," a requirement only permissible if the local school board determines that there is credible evidence that the home education is below the standards of the public school.

The judge . . . lamented the fact that [the law] upholds the rights of parents to home-school their children without interference from the government.

Laws Protect Home-Schoolers

Because of NJ's explicit laws protecting the parental right to educate their children at home, the judge had only limited options when it came to personally implementing his philosophies of "monitoring" and "registering" home-schoolers. The judge cautioned that, should the school board refuse to comply with his "suggestions", the court would "consider, by formal opinion, a request to join those parties to action."

The New Jersey Department of Education website states, "The provision, 'to receive equivalent instruction elsewhere than at school,' in N.J.S.A. 18A:38–25 permits parent(s)/guardian(s) to educate the child at home." According to New Jersey law, parents desiring to home-school their children are not required to submit any type of communication of intent to a local school board. Parents are also not required to have their home-school curricula approved by a school board.

An NJ school board may only act against a home-schooling parent "If there is credible evidence that the parent, guardian or other person having custody and control of a school-age child is not causing the child either to attend school (public or nonpublic) or to receive equivalent instruction elsewhere than at school . . ." Under those circumstances, the school board is permitted to request the parents/guardians of a school age child provide proof, such as a letter of intent, that the child is receiving "equivalent instruction."

Home-Schoolers Must Be Monitored

The judge criticized the NJ law and lamented the fact that it upholds the rights of parents to home-school their children without interference from the government. Implying that children being educated by their parents are unsupervised, the judge stated, "This is shocking to the court. In this day and age where we seek to protect children from harm and sexual predators, so many children are left unsupervised."

The judge continued, "In today's threatening world, where we seek to protect children from abuse, not just physical, but also educational abuse, how can we not monitor the educational welfare of all our children?" He then gave the case of a recently found starving child locked "in a putrid bedroom" as an example of what happens when home-schooled children are not "registered and supervised."

In what Bowman refers to as a "judicial temper tantrum" the judge opines, "This is not an attack against home schooling, but rather a statement that it is necessary to register those children for whom this alternative is chosen and to monitor that their educational needs are being adequately nurtured. Judicial interpretation of the statute requires such steps to measure 'equivalent instruction' when the alternative 'elsewhere than at school' is chosen by parents."

More Regulation or Oversight of Education Is Not Needed

Anne Basso

Anne Basso is a nurse and homeschooling mother.

Homeschooling debates come up from time to time on the message board that I belong to, and certain themes seem to repeat themselves. It's frustrating, at times, to have to defend something that I believe is a basic right that I have as a parent and something that I believe has been so good for our family and our children. Especially when I feel that the objections are well intentioned, but not especially well thought out. I thought I'd take a blog post and share a few.

Belief: Homeschoolers need more regulation because children could be abused.

Answer: Children are abused every day, all over this country, and the vast majority of them are in public schools. Many children have gone through public schools without their abuse being caught. So, obviously, if seeing a child *every day* is not a guarantee that they will not be abused, it seems unlikely that more paperwork or even occasional meetings with homeschooling families is unlikely to prevent or catch ongoing abuse.

Children spend 5 years in the care of their parents before going to school. It seems that to really get the government involved in stopping abuse, mandatory checks would be required for all children in all homes. Otherwise, homeschooling parents are being unfairly targeted.

Spotting child abuse is the work of an entire community. Not just teachers, but doctors, nurses, dentists, neighbors, and all sorts of people. Thinking that it's the school's responsibility

Anne Basso, "Regulating Homeschooling," *Our Homeschool.com (wordpress blog)*, August 29, 2007. Reproduced by permission.

to catch child abuse is not fair to the schools, and could allow the rest of us to think that it's not our responsibility when it is.

I see no proof that parents are having difficulty finding a curriculum or teaching it.

Belief: Parents haven't been trained. Oversight is needed to make sure that parents are getting the right curriculum and teaching it appropriately.

Answer: I believe that when discussing the need for more government intrusion into my life and that of my family, those proposing it have an obligation to prove that it is necessary. Now, I'll admit, as a Conservative, I'm likely going to bristle at the idea of more government to fix things. But even more so when it comes to my family. And I see no proof that parents are having difficulty finding a curriculum or teaching it. And if they are, there are a ton of resources within the homeschooling community with which to supplement or find something that works better. If the child is in public school and is being failed by the curriculum, they can't change it.

I don't believe that more government is going to help. I have too many public school teacher friends who are frustrated and annoyed by the "No Child Left Behind" laws which, though well intentioned, have gotten in the way of teachers actually teaching the students. Instead they have to teach to the test. That's what our increased regulations have given us in Public Schools. Not what I want in my home, thanks!

I already have to jump through more hoops than other parents because I don't have a college degree. Now, you can have a college degree in anything, not necessarily education, and it cuts down on what is required of you. And what's required of me that is different is that I provide grades (which I could just make up) and that I have my child tested yearly, though I don't have to share the results with the school district. So what's the point? I have four kids, a job, and I work hard to homeschool. I'm busy enough without having to jump through more hoops to prove myself to the school district.

There are quite a few oversights and regulations on public schools and yet children still fall through the cracks.

Belief: Homeschoolers need more oversight so that we can prevent students from falling through the educational cracks.

Answer: The truly awful homeschooling parent (whom I believe is rare but will concede exists) is not going to be deterred by such things as more regulation. They will simply move around and find new ways to avoid the regulations. Those punished will be homeschoolers like myself who are trying desperately to do everything right.

I don't think you can prevent some students from falling through the educational cracks. My father used to get students who, in High School, couldn't read. There are quite a few oversights and regulations on public schools and yet children still fall through the cracks. It's sad, and I don't like it, but I don't think more regulations for homeschoolers is the answer. Yet again, I think it must be proven that this is a problem within the homeschooling community and warrants such intrusion by the state and that such intrusion will make a difference. Less than 2% of America's students are homeschooled at all, so I can't see as there's a big epidemic.

Belief: It is our duty and obligation as a Democracy, and as a community to ensure that all children are educated, and that means making sure that homeschooled children meet certain expectations as well as public schooled children.

Answer: Our Founding Fathers believed that, for a Democracy, an educated populace was essential. However, they trusted the *parents* to provide that education as they saw fit. None of the Founding Fathers attended public schools, nor were they common in the United States until almost a century later. I will provide an education to my children, and I expect the *freedom* to do so as I see fit. Freedom being another idea that the Founding Fathers held dear.

I don't believe that it is the job of the community to raise my children. And if you're proposing greater demands or restrictions on me, I think you have to prove that it's necessary. But the research that I've read says that homeschooled children are more involved in the community, statistically speaking, than their [public] schooled counterparts:

> *Dr. Gary Knowles, of the University of Michigan, explored adults who were home educated. None were unemployed and none were on welfare, 94% said home education prepared them to be an independent person, 79% said it helped them interact with individuals from different levels of society, and they strongly supported the home education method. . . .*

Belief: If teachers have to jump through so many hoops, so should homeschoolers.

Answer: I am not asking to be paid government money to teach other people's children. I am actually paying taxes and spending my own money on top of that while educating my own children. I don't see how the two can be compared.

In the end, people are going to form their own opinions and have their own ideas about homeschooling, and I believe that those who advocate greater restrictions, oversights, or demands have the *best* of intentions. They really just want to make sure that kids are getting the education that they deserve. But, in my experience, the parents I've met *are* very concerned about their children's educations, and devoted to their learning. The community is vast, resourceful, and encouraging to one another. I don't think there's anything to be fixed with homeschooling, because I don't see any proof that it's broken.

I will never object to the state making resources available for those homeschoolers who wish to take advantage of them.

I will always object to their resources being forced upon me, or more government regulation and intrusion being the first resort for a problem that hasn't even been shown to exist.

Homeschooling Freedoms Must Be Maintained

Larry Kaseman and Susan Kaseman

Larry Kaseman and Susan Kaseman are executive directors of the Wisconsin Parents Association, a statewide grassroots organization dedicated to ensuring legislation does not limit homeschoolers' freedoms. The Kasemans also are columnists for Home Education Magazine.

Would you like to

- ensure that your family can make as many decisions as possible about the approach to homeschooling you will choose, the curriculum you will use, what you will do each day, and what principles and beliefs you will share with your children;

- make an important contribution to homeschooling both now and in the future; and

- learn more about taking responsibility for your own life and activities, lessons you can apply to other areas of your life?

You can do all this and more by following a few simple principles for maintaining homeschooling freedom. . . .

Homeschooling is complicated enough when we just focus on our own families. It takes time, energy, and experience to organize our lives around the fact that we are homeschooling, choose an approach that has a reasonable chance of working for each child, gather materials we need, defend our sanity when questioned by friends and relatives, and keep our own doubts under control. Add to this the mid-course corrections that need to be made because we discover a better approach or our children outgrow what we've been doing and are ready for something new. It sometimes seems like focusing on our own family is all we have time or energy to do.

Working to Maintain Freedoms

But we make a big mistake if we don't put some time and energy into working to maintain our homeschooling freedoms. Unless we work to ensure that state regulation of homeschooling is not increased, critics and opponents of homeschooling (such as some school officials, social workers, legislators, teachers unions, etc.) are likely to increase it. If this were to happen, our own homeschooling would be much more difficult. We'd be more limited in what we could do. For example, state requirements that we submit our curriculum for review end approval, have our children take standardized tests, or send periodic reports to public school officials tend to undermine our confidence in our ability to choose an approach to homeschooling that will work for our family and follow it. We become handicapped and may have to spend more time complying with state requirements and figuring out ways to homeschool according to our principles and beliefs despite the requirements. To be sure, many families homeschool successfully in states that have such requirements, but it is more difficult. Homeschoolers who have to work with public school standards (by adopting a curriculum that public school officials approve, or reporting to public school officials, or taking tests based on conventional school curriculum, etc.) often have a more difficult time discovering and creating approaches to homeschooling that will allow their children to interact with the real world and prepare for adult life than they would have if they were free of such regulations and could simply concentrate on their children's educations. It's much better to include plans to work to maintain our homeschooling freedoms with our other activities as homeschoolers. When conventional schools are beginning a new academic year is a good time to review what we are doing to maintain our freedoms or to begin working to maintain our freedoms if we're new to homeschooling or to this idea.

But, you may be thinking, isn't maintaining our freedoms dull, onerous, difficult, sometimes hopeless work? Not at all! Most of the time, all that we have to do is to be alert and make sensible choices as we go about homeschooling our own families. The few specific steps we need to take, outlined below, are relatively quick and easy, provide great learning opportunities, increase our confidence, and help us learn to take responsibility for ourselves, something we can use throughout our lives. The work is especially manageable if every homeschooler does their part. The only major time- end energy-consuming work is dealing with a crisis, like countering legislation that undermines our freedom. Fortunately, such crises do not occur often and are much less likely to occur if we (and other homeschoolers) have followed the basic points outlined below.

Any action that exceeds statutes or regulations sets a precedent.

Here Are Eight Essential Principles

1. Know what is required of homeschoolers in your state. Have a copy of the homeschooling statutes and/or regulations available for reference in case you need it. You may be able to get a copy from a statewide homeschooling organization, a local support group, or an experienced homeschooler in your state. In addition, be sure to ask experienced homeschoolers how the statutes or regulations are enforced. Enforcement may not follow the letter of the law, and it's important to know what your choices and risks are. Don't ask school officials or

the state department of education for information about statutes, regulations, or what is required. They often do not know, have been misinformed, or misunderstand what the statutes or regulations say. Be careful about information from books or web sites that cover the laws in all 50 states. They sometimes provide only the text of the statutes without crucial information about how they are interpreted or enforced. The best source of information is knowledgeable, experienced homeschoolers who live in the state you're interested in.

2. Do only the minimum required by statute or regulation. If a school official asks or tells you to do more than is required, politely refuse and explain what is required. If they persist, ask them to show the statute or regulation that gives them the authority to make such a request. Occasionally, it may be tempting to exceed the minimum requirements of the law by showing school officials our curriculums, samples of our children's accomplishments, test scores, etc. even though these are not required by statute in our state [Wisconsin]. Perhaps we are proud of our children's accomplishments or want to educate officials about homeschooling or show them how well it works. It is very important to resist such temptation. Any action that exceeds statutes or regulations sets a precedent. It's likely to increase demands officials make of us and other homeschoolers in the future. It also may increase the questions, doubts, concerns, and criticisms that officials have about our homeschooling. Requirements vary greatly from state to state. Be careful not to do more than the minimum required in your state.

3. Don't ignore violations of your rights even if they seem too small to matter. Major freedoms are sometimes lost one small step at a time. Our failure to respond also encourages those who are limiting our freedoms to con-

tinue the process. For example, suppose a school district requires that homeschoolers submit their test scores, even though the statutes in the state do not give districts the authority to require them. If homeschoolers do not object, in a while the district may ask for copies of homeschoolers' curriculums in addition to their test scores. On the other hand, if homeschoolers object strongly the first time the district exceeds its authority (either by mistake or in a deliberate attempt to increase its power and authority over homeschoolers), school officials will probably be more reluctant to take on homeschoolers in the future. Responding to small infringements of our freedoms not only prevents loss of freedom in the specific situation in question. It also prevents future, perhaps more serious, such challenges. People who think that homeschoolers shouldn't complain as long as no one declares homeschooling illegal greatly misunderstand the importance of choosing an approach to education and a curriculum, allowing children to pursue their interest and learn at their own pace, and offering our children an education consistent with our principles and beliefs rather than those of the public school system.

4. Do not seek or accept any benefits from the government, including direct funding, tax deductions, or tax credits. Work to prevent the government from offering money or favors to any homeschoolers. There is no such thing as a free lunch. Such benefits are likely to be followed by increased regulation, especially since the government is accountable for how tax dollars are spent. Even benefits that seem quite safe, like allowing homeschoolers to play on public school sports teams, open the door for increased regulation of homeschooling. Such regulation would apply to all homeschoolers; families could not refuse the benefit and avoid the increased

regulation. It is important to remember that there are people and organizations (for example, some school official, social workers, legislators, teachers unions, etc.) who are looking for opportunities to increase state regulation of homeschooling.

5. Do not push for new homeschooling legislation except in very unusual situations. Small minorities generally have difficulty getting legislation passed, especially if they don't have large sums of money to hire lobbyists. In addition, once a bill has been introduced, it is very difficult to control. It can be changed so much through amendments that it actually ends up the opposite of what it started out to be. Some of the best homeschooling laws in the country have resulted from legislation introduced by opponents of homeschooling being changed through amendment. It is easier for a small minority like homeschoolers to gain support from non-homeschoolers when we are a beleaguered minority being put upon by a large interest group like a teachers union than to find support for legislation we initiated ourselves.

6. Stay out of court if at all possible. It is almost always better for homeschoolers to try to reach settlements through negotiation or arbitration than to take cases to court. Rulings in court cases generally uphold the status quo and support the dominant culture. This means that rulings concerning small minorities such as homeschoolers tend to be biased in favor of conventional education rather than alternatives. We are much better off without any court rulings than with rulings that go against us. Evidence to support this idea can be found in a 1990 report written by Jane Henkel of the Wisconsin Legislative Council titled "Recent Court Cases Examining the Constitutionality of Other States' Laws Regulating Home Schools." Her report showed that court cases tend to

uphold the constitutionality of state regulation of home-schooling. The report states, "Special care was taken to attempt to find reported cases striking down state regulations. With the limited exception of cases which found regulations to be unconstitutionally vague, that effort was unsuccessful, which tends to indicate that there are few, if any, such cases." The report is available at http://www.homeedmag.com/HEM/185/henkel/info_memo90-23.html or from the Wisconsin Legislative Council, One East Main Street, Suite 401, Madison, WI 53703, (608) 266–1304.

7. Understand and apply the distinction between compulsory school attendance and compulsory education. Basically, remember and remind school officials and others that the law requires that young people attend school, but it does not require that they receive an education while doing so. Therefore, it is discriminatory for school officials, judges, court commissioners, and others to insist that homeschoolers demonstrate that their children are receiving an education that is equivalent to the education that children supposedly receive in public schools or that they are at grade level or penalize them for failing to achieve specific educational goals. For more information, see the recent Taking Charge column, "Don't Let Compulsory Attendance Turn into Compulsory Education," available at http://www.homeedmag.com/HEM/224/jatch.html. . . .

8. Work with other homeschoolers. Some of homeschooling's greatest strengths stem from the fact that it is a grassroots movement. It becomes even stronger as we communicate with each other, share information and experiences, support each other, and work together to maintain our freedoms.

If your state has a statewide inclusive grassroots home-schooling organization, consider supporting it. Such organizations have contributed enormously to the work that has been done to maintain homeschooling freedoms. Become a member, make a donation, purchase materials, and attend their conferences. It is very important to be organized and prepared before challenges to our freedoms arise. Such organizations are also a very good way to connect with other homeschoolers.

Also consider joining a local homeschooling support group. If none exists in your area, start one yourself. It can be as simple as getting together with one or two other families for whatever activities you choose.

Conclusion

There's no doubt about it: the choices we can make about how we will homeschool each day are influenced by what our state requires of homeschoolers. As homeschoolers, we need to take responsibility for preventing an increase in state regulation and an accompanying loss of homeschooling freedom. No one else will maintain our freedoms for us; in fact, a number of individuals and groups are continually looking for ways to increase state regulation of homeschooling. Fortunately, working to maintain our freedom is not difficult or time-consuming, especially if each of us does our part. It does require understanding some fundamental principles, including those discussed [above], and keeping them in mind as we go about our homeschooling. Don't let the rest of us down. Do your part. Make a significant contribution to the present and future of homeschooling.

Parents Can Legally Instruct Their Children

Deborah Stevenson

Deborah Stevenson, mother of two grown children, Samantha and Cassandra, realized that homeschooling is what all parents do from the time children are born, and that it was a natural thing to continue to do so. So she did. Deborah became involved in legal work as a result of homeschooling her children. She became involved in protecting her right to homeschool as a parent before she began attending law school. She homeschooled, as well as drove her children to college, where they took courses during the day, and went to law school at night. She currently practices education law and appellate law privately in addition to working as executive director of National Home Education Legal Defense (NHELD), LLC. Ms. Stevenson formed Connecticut Citizens to Uphold the Right to Educate (C.U.R.E.) in 1989 in order to assist all parents in the state to retain their right to instruct their children at home without government interference. Because she believed in the Tenth Amendment's provision that all powers not specifically granted to the federal government belong to the states and to the people, C.U.R.E. remained a state organization protecting the rights of citizens in the state. It was not until 2003, when Deborah realized that there was a continuing effort by another organization to actively promote the adoption of federal regulation of homeschooling, that she decided to form NHELD. A national organization was necessary in order to inform and assist parents in all states in halting federal regulation and retaining authority in the states to instruct their children in freedom. Ms. Stevenson has an extensive background as a public speaker. She spent ten years as a reporter interviewing all sorts of interesting people from parents to presidents. She also hosted many radio programs on a variety of topics throughout her ten

Deborah Stevenson, "One Parent's Demand for the Truth About the Legality of Homeschooling," *Family Times*, May/June 2006. Reproduced by permission.

year career. She has conducted many workshops on homeschooling and the law. You can find articles that Ms. Stevenson has published in Home Education Magazine, Home Educator's Family Times, *and on NHELD's Web site, www.nheld.com, to name a few.*

Nothing makes me angrier than a lie, except when a lie is repeated so often that people believe it to be truth. I'm sick of lies, distorted truth, spin, and revisionist history. Can we just get back to reality? Can we just hold people accountable for their purposeful distortions?

Can we just set the record straight?

Homeschooling Is an Age-Old Custom

The lie that makes me the angriest is the lie that "It's legal to homeschool 'now.'" The implication in that statement is the lie. The implication is that it wasn't legal to homeschool before, or that homeschooling only became legal in the past 20 years or so. Nothing could be farther from the truth.

At no time during the growth of the public school system . . . did state governments declare the instruction of children by their parents to be illegal.

What is "homeschooling?" It is the act of parents undertaking their responsibility to instruct their own children. This is the most basic, the most natural, the most instinctive undertaking of the human race. Since the beginning of the human race, whether you accept the scientific view that man lived as early as seven million years ago or whether you accept the religious view that God created man four or five thousand years ago, the inescapable fact is that parents have instructed their children from the moment of birth to adulthood since the inception of the human race whenever that was. It wasn't illegal to do so in the beginning, and it's not illegal to do so now.

What is "new" is the public school system. The first public school in America was established by Puritan settlers in Boston in 1635. It was established by the Reverend John Cotton who wanted to create a school modeled after the Free Grammar School in England, in which Latin and Greek were taught. The truth is, though, that the opening of that first public school did not automatically mean that the instruction of children by their parents somehow automatically became illegal. Quite the opposite is true.

In the early days in New England, in fact, parents were expected to instruct their children. If parents didn't instruct their children such that the children became "unruly", the selectmen of the town could take the child from the parent and place the child, not with government officials, but with another surrogate parent of sorts called a master. It then became the master's responsibility to instruct the child.

It is important to note that the compulsory attendance laws were aimed at those children who were not being educated by other means.

A Compulsory Attendance Law Adopted

Over time, small public schools were opened, many of which were operated and overseen by ecclesiastical societies. Oversight slowly gave way to oversight by towns and, later, to what we now know as boards of education. At no time during the growth of the public school system, however, did state governments declare the instruction of children by their parents to be illegal.

The popularity of the public school system increased dramatically during the nineteenth century, thanks in large part to [educator] Horace Mann. He persuaded the Massachusetts legislature, in fact, to set up a six-month minimum school year and led a movement to set up teacher institutions throughout the state. Even while Mann was tending to this task, the Massachusetts legislature at no time declared the instruction of children by their parents to be illegal.

As the public school system grew, legislatures adopted more laws about the system. The law that most people are familiar with that state legislatures adopted is the "compulsory attendance" law. This law has many permutations depending on the state in which it was adopted. Its basic thrust is to tell parents that their children "must attend" public school. Massachusetts was the first state to enact such a law in 1852.

It required children between the ages of eight and fourteen to attend school for at least three months each year.

Instructing Your Children Is Not Illegal

The compulsory attendance laws, for the most part, initially were adopted during the height of the industrial revolution in the nineteenth century. This was a time when the growth of industry opened new sources of income for families. It was a time when parents allowed their children to work in the factories, instead of on the family farms of yesteryear. For a multitude of reasons, those in power deemed it inherently injurious to the children to work in the factories, and, instead deemed it eminently more important for them to attend public school. By 1918 all states followed suit. It is important to note that the compulsory attendance laws were aimed at those children who were not being educated by other means. In fact, there were many exemptions to these laws. Most importantly, these laws simply did not apply to those children who were being educated by other means. In other words, the legislatures did not declare education of children by their parents, or by private schools or tutors for that matter, to be illegal.

Today, most states still have "compulsory attendance laws". *But that does not necessarily mean that it was ever illegal for parents to instruct their own children. The truth is, it was never "illegal"* for parents to instruct their own *children*. Can we please stop perpetuating the lie that it was illegal?

It is the development of this "new" public school system that, in part, has fueled the lie. The public school system has become so huge and so powerful that it dominates the public's thinking. It is also the agenda of some to perpetuate the lie. The lie benefits different groups such as the established public school system or established organizations purporting to "assist" parents fearful of the public school system taking their rights away.

Government Has Limited Authority

What is true is that many states did, and still do, impose government regulations on how and when parents instruct their children. It is unfortunate that the government imposes any regulations on parents who instruct their own children. It is my belief, however, that one of the reasons why the government has been successful in adopting regulations affecting the right of parents to instruct their children is because the lie that it was illegal for parents to homeschool in the first place has been perpetuated for so long. From this lie flows a host of issues. For example, if you believe the lie that it was illegal for parents to instruct their children, it follows that parents would have to seek "permission" from the government in order to do so. If you believe the lie, it follows that parents would be fearful that they would not receive that "permission." If you believe the lie, it follows that parents would be grateful when the government magnanimously grants that "permission." If you believe the lie, it follows that parents are more apt to see "regulation" of parental instruction by the government as a matter of course. After all, if the government has the "authority" to grant "permission" to parents to instruct, certainly the government has the "authority" to impose "regulation" of parents' ability to instruct, and it is reasonable for the government to do so.

Armed with the facts, armed with the truth, however, parents can begin to realize that, in reality, the government never did have the "authority" to declare the right of parents to instruct their children as illegal, and it's a safe bet that the government in your state never did declare the right of parents to instruct their children as illegal.

CHAPTER 4

Should Homeschooled Children Have Access to Public School Resources?

Chapter Preface

The great majority of homeschooled children are very happy with their educational lifestyle and do not feel they are missing anything by not attending public or private schools. Some, however, want to enjoy both worlds. They would like to continue to be home-educated but at the same time be able to attend certain public school classes, play on public school athletic teams, or play an instrument in a school band. This is especially true of high school-age students.

In recent years an increasing number of states have been more amenable to allowing more participation. In 2007, the High School Legal Defense Association (HSLDA) reported that eighteen states—Arizona, Colorado, Florida, Idaho, Iowa, Maine, Michigan, Minnesota, New Hampshire, New Mexico, Nebraska, North Dakota, Oregon, Pennsylvania, Utah, Vermont, Washington, and Wyoming—had statutes that authorized some form of public school access by homeschooled students. Arizona and Oregon required school districts to allow access to interscholastic activities only.

In those states without such statutes, it generally falls to school districts or local school boards to set a policy. Local boards often turn for input to state athletic associations, which tend not to want to allow homeschoolers equal access to public school athletics. Very few state high school athletic associations have adopted by-laws that allow homeschoolers to play on public school sports teams.

Even in those states that do have laws allowing homeschoolers to participate in public school programs, certain requirements must be met. These vary from one state to another but typically mandate that the homeschooler must be in compliance with the state homeschool law, meet the same eligibility requirements as public school students, and provide test scores or academic reports that prove he or she is passing his or her core subjects.

Even though a growing number of states are permitting homeschoolers to take part in at least some public school extracurricular activities, the issue of equal access remains problematic from a number of perspectives. It continues to be a subject of debate among homeschoolers themselves. Many oppose equal access because they believe pushing for access laws will lead to more government regulation of homeschoolers. Some homeschooling parents take another position, choosing often reluctantly to allow an athletically talented child to enroll in public high school so he or she can play on the school team where there is sufficient competition to showcase his or her talent—and hopefully win an athletic scholarship to college. Other homeschoolers and their advocates across the nation have reacted to the issue by choosing to start homeschooler athletic associations, leagues, and teams, whose numbers continue to grow. Homeschoolers can derive satisfaction from the fact that their efforts, the growth and success of their teams, and the talents of their athletes have not gone unnoticed. According to a 2008 article in the *New York Times*, "Only a decade ago, home-school athletics was considered little more than organized recess for children without traditional classrooms. Now, home-school players are tracked by scouts, and dozens of them have accepted scholarships to colleges as small as Blue Mountain in Mississippi and as well known as Iowa State."

Participation of Homeschoolers in Public School Extracurricular Activities Should Be Allowed

State of Pennsylvania

The following is a news release posted on the state of Pennsylvania's official Web site, http://PA.gov, which provides news and information related to the state of Pennsylvania.

Governor Edward G. Rendell [on November 2005] signed Senate Bill 361, sponsored by Sen. Bob Regola (R-Westmoreland), into law to help the state's 25,000 children who are taught at home participate in extracurricular activities in their local school districts.

"While I have long been an advocate of public education and the need to ensure a world-class public education system in our state, I think the commitment to education demonstrated by homeschool parents has too long been undervalued," said Governor Rendell in his signing letter to the legislature.

"As Senate Bill 361 worked its way through the Legislature, I asked my staff to review such critical questions as the financial implications of the bill, whether it imposes any new financial burdens and whether such burdens could be met with current resources. I also asked that we consider the appropriateness of state legislation given the local control structure of Pennsylvania's school system. This thorough review process gave me an opportunity to understand the personal circumstances and the goals of homeschool parents and their children."

"Governor Rendell Says Home-Schooled Children Can Participate in School District Extracurricular Activities," in State of Pennsylvania's Governor's Office, November 2005.

"I read of Barry Clay's desire for his children to participate with their friends in extracurricular activities in the Carlisle Area School District, of Carol Loys' hope that her children could do the same with their friends in the West Shore School District, and of Beverly Wiezorek's efforts to convince the Pittsburgh School District to let her son, Wesley, play football. These were just a few examples that illustrated the pleas of parents, asking that their children be able to enjoy the benefit of extracurricular sports, the opportunity to compete for college sports scholarships and the ability to participate in and contribute to their communities."

[Homeschool] parents deserve our respect and their children are entitled to be included in the activities of their school district.

Inclusion Is Appropriate

"I found it disheartening that 221 of our school districts do not permit homeschool children to engage in school sports, plays, clubs or other programs that promote good social values, integrate our communities and clearly contribute to the positive social development of our children. I agree with these dedicated parents that they have every right to be frustrated. As any good parent would, they are looking out for the interests of their children. And not only are they involved in their child's education, they share in their local school's cost by paying property taxes. It seems disingenuous to suggest that permitting these students to take part in school-based extracurricular activities would be unjust or a burden on public school budgets since their parents are paying property taxes."

"It's clear that parents who homeschool their children do not make this decision lightly. Some do so because they want their child's education to be integrated with their faith and do not have access to a private school that reflects their religious beliefs. Others choose homeschooling in an effort to offer more challenging coursework to children who have advanced beyond the available curricula offered locally. Others may have a child with special needs and opt for homeschooling as a way to provide individualized attention that may be unavailable or impractical for their school district. These parents make tough choices, rearranging their lives entirely around the needs of their children. These parents deserve our respect and their children are entitled to be included in the activities of their school district."

Senate Bill 361 amends the Public School Code of 1949. As of Jan. 1, 2006, a school district of residence must permit a child enrolled in a home education program to participate in any extracurricular activities provided by that local district. The child must meet both eligibility and the activities' try-out requirements. The child will also have to comply with the rules of the club or organization he or she chooses to join.

Interscholastic athletics and activities, which occur between schools within the district or between schools outside of the district, are also included this amendment. If the activity requires a physical exam or medical test, the district must post the information on their web site and circulate it in an area publication.

The bill passed the Senate 34-16 and the House, with amendments, 197-2. The Senate concurred, with additional amendments, 33-17. The House agreed 195-3. The bill is effective immediately.

Homeschoolers Deserve Equal Access to Extracurricular Activities

Alabama EqualAccess

Alabama EqualAccess is a group of concerned Alabama citizens who united to lobby for the passage of a bill to allow home-schoolers equal access to interscholastic sports and other extra-curricular activities.

We offer the following Q&A topics but none of the answers make any difference, regardless of how true the facts may be, if the reader is biased against homeschoolers to begin with. The reader must first ask themselves if they believe that all student-athletes of our state deserve an equal opportunity to participate in extracurricular activities. That is the bottom line. Let us keep in mind as a state that a student is a student—regardless of where they receive their education. Each child is already a part of our society. Turning out the best equipped individuals should be the goal of us all. Some states, such as Florida, wisely offer an almost complete *cafeteria-style* approach for home-schoolers where the parents get to choose not only public school extracurricular activities but also academic subjects such as science, music, math, or other classes that their child needs. As frightening as that prospect may seem for many entrenched public educators, the reality is that it works out very well. Studies also prove that states which allow equal access, like Minnesota, who is ranked number one academically according to the ALEC [American Legislative Exchange Council] study, are consistently ranked in the top academic performance states.

Alabama EqualAccess, "The State of Alabama's Tim Tebow Bill: Frequently Asked Questions and Answers," *www.timtebowbill.com*, 2006. Copyright © 2006 TimTebow Bill.com. Reproduced by permission.

Regardless, the system should not get in the way of what is best for the student. School administrators and coaches are some of the hardest working and most conscientious people in our state. They have constant demands on them from all sides whether it be teachers, other employees, the state education system, the Federal government, unions, parents, and last but not least the students. They are to be commended for their diligence. They need to realize though that equal access is not a problem waiting to happen to them but rather a wonderful opportunity to add a few great students and parents to the *team*. Not just the school sports team but the overall school team, the community *team*. All the negative thoughts that come to mind for an administrator simply have not materialized in the 23 other states that permit equal access. We encourage administrators not to be so caught up in the past or in the demands of the present that they forget what our schools are supposed to be about. . . .

We are all citizens . . . with hopefully the same goal in mind and that is to provide the best for our children.

Cost Should Not Be a Factor

- *What is the cost?*

Most school teams will not add extra positions for a sport or band to accommodate homeschoolers so the cost is nil in this case. Some schools may choose to add extra positions on a team or individual sport. However, typically it is the booster clubs that raise the lion's share of the athletic money spent. It is likely that homeschool parents would be some of the most enthusiastic supporters of a booster club!

The answer to the cost issue also depends on if the schools decide to count a *partial* student. What is not pointed out by the opposition is that Alabama spends on average about $6,300 per student per year. The state's 25,000 or more homeschoolers save the taxpayers approximately $157,500,000 *each* year in state and Federal funds by not requiring public school services! Below is a fitting quote from a letter from a dedicated homeschool mom, Marcia Guyse, who holds a masters degree and is a certified teacher who taught for years in the Alabama and Texas school systems:

A homeschooled student is a student . . . just the same as a public or private schooled student and therefore deserves equal and fair treatment.

"If we as educators truly want what is best for the student, then we will include all students, including home-schooled students. A new day is dawning for education. In states like Minnesota, whose educational program is ranked number one in the nation, parents can choose the best path for the education of their children, whether it be public schools, private schools, charter schools, or home schools. The state does not penalize them for this choice by excluding them from any services, but state funds actually follow the child to the school that is chosen. Presently, those 25,000 home schoolers in the State of Alabama are saving the state a $6,300 per student expenditure. [Alabama Education Association executive secretary] Dr. Paul Hubbert is worried about the "cost" of passing this legislation. Couldn't just a little of that money follow those students to a school's sports or music program? It's time for educators [and teacher's unions] to quit worrying about economic and political costs of education and start thinking of the cost of not offering the best educational opportunities to all students in Alabama." . . .

Homeschoolers Deserve Equal Treatment

• *What does "extracurricular activities" encompass?*

This has been addressed in the rewritten [Tim Tebow] bill. The bill includes only sports and band. As homeschoolers already participate at some local public schools in certain extra-curricular activities such as music, it seems that individual local schools have already decided that allowing certain students to participate in certain areas already produces a win-win situation. This bill does not seek to limit that opportunity for homeschool students that live in a district that *already* permits such activity. The bill would even-out the opportunity and make it more fair as it would apply to all students regardless of school zone. . . .

- *"If our sports are good enough for you then why not our academics"*?

This is an old argument with inherent bias against home-schoolers. First of all there is no "you" nor "our" to this issue. We are all citizens of this state with hopefully the same goal in mind and that is to provide the best for our children. This is about what is *best* for the student—not what is merely *good enough*. A homeschooled student is a student in this state just the same as a public or private schooled student and therefore deserves equal and fair treatment—especially by the state-sponsored educational establishment. This should apply to athletics as well as academics. A child can freely walk into any school in this state in the district where they legally reside and obtain educational services. This should not exclude extracurricular activities that are offered by that school. Many who exhibit this attitude often have the misconceived notion that homeschoolers think they are "better" than others. While this notion may be the case in some instances, the same could be said of public-schoolers. So it simply points out a bias or resentment towards homeschoolers. Again it has nothing to do with the intelligent debate that many on both sides of this issue are trying to conduct. Those who choose to continue to hold this attitude should realize at least that this *is* an instance where homeschoolers are offering an olive branch and trying to reach out to the public school system.

- *Illegal Immigrants and Exchange Students have more rights than homeschoolers in this regard!*

On a side note, it is blatantly unfair to many citizens that illegal immigrants to our great country and state can enroll their children, technically, the day they move into a district and receive all benefits offered to any other student. This participation includes the right to participate in extracurricular activities. This applies to foreign exchange students as well. Even they have more rights than our state's very own homeschoolers. Homeschool families, many of whom have been upstanding, legal, tax-paying citizens of this state for decades, are excluded. Is this fair?...

Participation in a comprehensive extracurricular and academic program contributes to student development of the social and intellectual skills necessary to become a well-rounded adult.

Children's Best Interest

- *Is this going to allow the government to interfere with the rights of homeschoolers?*

This is a voluntary opportunity only for homeschoolers who fill out a form and request to be involved in the program. It will have no effect on other homeschoolers who wish not to be bothered.

We homeschoolers are indeed an independent bunch! We homeschoolers who support this legislation understand the battle that had to be fought nationwide to be able to exercise the God-given responsibility and the right to educate our children at home if we deemed it best for the student. But frankly that is a past battle; it will not be fought again. We won! Homeschooling is well accepted as part of the educational options for many citizens. While it will take the educational "system" a while to accept this, it is occurring. I'm afraid that in our zeal for homeschooling, we often forget that it is not about the right to do this or do that but *it is about what is best for each child* that is important. . . .

Interscholastic extracurricular activities are an important complement to the academic curriculum. Participation in a comprehensive extracurricular and academic program contributes to student development of the social and intellectual skills necessary to become a well-rounded adult.

Many extracurricular activities can be provided to students on an individual basis, such as tennis, golf, piano lessons or art. However, some sports or activities require groups of students and cannot be achieved on an individual basis.

Options Afforded by Public Education

Children have different gifts. Not all can or want to play football or baseball, but each deserves to have the opportunity to develop his or her talents.

Most of us have been involved in homeschool teams and have seen many other great examples of valiant efforts by great homeschoolers to field teams of excellence. But let's be honest, short of Bill Gates joining the movement, do we think we could ever fund sports programs to the level necessary to bring them up to the caliber of most of the public and private school teams? While we know full well that there is more to athletics than funding and visibility, it is nonetheless an important part. And what about continuity of the program and coaches? Homeschoolers don't have the options afforded by public schools in this regard. . . .

Again, this option is available at some level in over 20 states already and we have not found one state that experienced adverse effects or instances where the freedom or rights of homeschoolers have been harmed. In 2006 when a local Pennsylvania school tried to "retest" a homeschooled athlete they were quick to drop the requirement when confronted by facts from the HSLDA [Homeschool Legal Defense Association].

HSLDA also states, in the states where equal access laws have been passed, there has not been one case where additional laws have been passed that affect the homeschool population of that state. . . .

Public schools do not "own" competitive athletics; they belong to the students, their families, and the residents of Alabama.

Discrimination Against Homeschoolers

- *Religious Discrimination imposed by a "State Actor" - A very real argument with a Supreme Court precedent:*

Just as the Alabama legislature has decided that public schools do not hold a monopoly on education, so the AHSAA [Alabama High School Athletic Association] should not hold a monopoly on competitive athletics.

The AHSAA is a private organization which governs all middle and high school competitive athletics in Alabama and discriminates against certain classes of students based on their educational choice.

It is time for the State Legislature to require the AHSAA to stop discriminating against students because of an educational choice. Students taught at home under a church school covering or by a private tutor cannot participate in athletics because a private organization, acting on behalf of the State, prohibits their participation.

The SUPREME COURT OF THE UNITED STATES in the *BRENTWOOD ACADEMY v. TENNESSEE SECONDARY SCHOOL ATHLETIC ASSOCIATION et al.* stated in the opinion of February 20, 2001, "Save for the Sixth Circuit, every Court of Appeals to consider a statewide athletic association like this one has found it to be a *state actor*".

Whether the AHSAA is a statutory agency of the State is immaterial because the AHSAA fulfills a certain function on behalf of the State for public schools. Just as public schools and governments are not allowed by federal law to discriminate against students based on race, sex, religion, the AHSAA as a "State Actor" cannot discriminate either. Therefore, the State of Alabama has given parents the right to teach their children under a church school covering and must allow these students based on their religious choice of schooling to participate in competitive athletics.

Children Should Not Be Penalized

Public schools do not "own" competitive athletics; they belong to the students, their families, and the residents of Alabama. It is just as much in the interest of the State of Alabama to help students in private and church schools to develop to their full potential as students in the public schools. The Legislature should not allow such a discriminatory practice to take place. The AHSAA is, in essence, a private exclusive club, which permits only certain students in Alabama to enjoy the privilege of group activities because of the schools they attend.

At least 23 other states recognize the importance of extracurricular activities in the development of a child. Alabama needs to do what is in the best interest of all children. All parents pay taxes to support the free public education system, but their children are penalized because they chose a different path to education. Education is a requirement for Alabama children. Extracurricular activities is a privilege and should be an opportunity for all children, not just those who attend a public school.

Homeschoolers Have the Right to Participate in After-School Activities

Provo Daily Herald

The Provo Daily Herald *is a daily newspaper in Provo, Utah.*

Do home-schoolers have as much right as any other kid to take part in a school district's after-school activities? Of course.

This has been a topic of growing interest since Florida quarterback Tim Tebow, who was home-schooled, won the Heisman Trophy.

Sen. Mark Madsen, R-Eagle Mountain, [Utah,] has introduced bills to clarify the right of charter, online and home-schooled students to take part in extracurricular activities at public schools, tailoring the language to address criticisms. He would restrict students to extracurricular activities at schools they otherwise would have attended, or schools they attended in the past. Madsen has also crafted a fair funding formula.

The proposal should be passed. The parents of home-schoolers pay taxes to support the schools, even as their kids impose no expense burden whatsoever on classrooms, labs or anywhere else. The programs we're talking about fall outside the regular curriculum—they're not necessary for graduation. They're extras, as the term *extracurricular* implies.

It's only fair that these families get something for their tax money.

Backers of ballroom dance, athletics, the performing arts and other extracurricular activities rightfully trumpet the value of such programs, which enrich lives, build character,

"In Our View: Let Home-School Kids Participate," *Daily Herald*, January 27, 2008. Reproduced by permission.

promote teamwork and keep kids out of trouble. Those attributes are exactly why the programs should be available to everybody.

If a kid is not a top performer academically, but a gifted athlete, why should he be prevented from developing that gift which he does possess?

Grades Should Not Be an Issue

A legislative committee has held up Madsen's proposal so that its backers can add requirements that home-schoolers' academic progress be monitored by third parties.

Opponents have conjured up a nightmare—unrealistic, in our view—that some parents will claim home-school status so that their budding superstars won't be barred from a team on account of poor grades. We suppose this could happen in theory, but it is no reason to block Madsen's proposal. The question should not turn on the rarest of exceptions.

Besides, it's fair to ask: If a kid is not a top performer academically, but a gifted athlete, why should he be prevented from developing that gift which he does possess? This question should be answered one of these days.

Madsen bridles at the suggestion that parents would resort to fraud. "Somehow every parent is suspect, and a closet perjurer ready to abandon their honor so that their kids can participate in extracurricular activities," he said.

It's not even a matter of honor. Utah parents generally want their kids in public school. End of story.

Third-Party Verification

If amendments are needed to Madsen's bills, they should be modest. Lawmakers should not erect major barriers to solve minor theoretical flaws. Athletes are simply not going to leave the hallowed halls of local high schools en masse to be home-schooled.

As for qualifying grades, the Legislature should move equally gently. So long as home-school is recognized as a valid, legal option for education in the State of Utah, it follows that measurement of whether a student is academically qualified to participate in extracurricular activity should flow from the home school, just as it flows from the public school for a public school student.

As a rule, parents who choose home-schooling for their kids are highly motivated; and home-schooled students tend to perform at high levels. Thus, requiring third-party verification of a home-schooled kid's academic standing is pretty much a waste of effort. Worse, it's an intrusion on the prerogatives of home-school educators (the parents) who are operating within the bounds of state law.

The "grade check" strikes us as a political nod to the public education establishment, which thrives on bureaucracy. But paperwork should not be confused with actual outcomes. After all, even graduation from a public high school is no guarantee of intelligence or future success. Home-school actually delivers better odds.

Cost Issues

As for costs associated with the inclusion of home-schooled students in extracurricular activities, the main costs are already sunk in stadiums, training equipment, pools, basketball courts and more. Coaches have been hired. A few extra kids trying out for a team or choir will have negligible—if not zero—impact on finances. Most extracurricular programs also require the payment of fees for participation.

But let's go back to Tim Tebow. As a high school quarterback, he had 95 passing touchdowns and scored 62 running. Let's imagine the next Tim Tebow is being home-schooled in Utah County right now. Why shouldn't he be allowed to play?

There is simply no link between any extracurricular program and the style of academic instruction a kid is getting in other parts of the school day.

And again, home-schoolers are taxpayers. Their tax dollars have purchased the right for their children to participate.

Allowing Access to Public School Resources May Harm Homeschooling

Valerie Delp

Valerie Delp is a senior blogger for families.com, a blog network for family topics.

One heated issue in homeschooling is whether or not homeschoolers should be allowed equal access to public school's "extras." Should a homeschooled student get to use the local school's computer lab, or library? Should they have the right to text books or AP [advanced placement] classes if they choose to use them? Many schools and districts allow this sharing of materials with homeschoolers, even if there are no state laws that mandate them to do so. However, the debate heats up when people start talking about extracurricular activities. Should homeschooled students be allowed to play sports on school teams or what about join the debate team or chess club?

Proponents of Equal Access Legislation point out that homeschooling families pay taxes to support public schools. Many families feel that their children miss out on opportunities, particularly in the area of athletics, because they don't have a chance to play. This would apply to students who are gifted athletes for example, that can't get "scouted" by a college because they're not playing.

Eligibility Guidelines Vary

I am likely in a minority as a homeschooling parent but I am not generally in favor of allowing homeschooled students access to public school resources. Homeschooling, like private

Valerie Delp, "Equal Access Laws for Homeschoolers," *families.com*, July 30, 2006. Reproduced by permission.

school, is a choice. Every schooling choice comes with pros and cons and I feel like homeschoolers need to find other ways to get what they need rather than turning to the public school. Using public school resources comes with strings attached that can affect the entire homeschooling community. There are enough resources out there now that homeschoolers can have access to necessary materials without going through the public school for them.

Something that many homeschooling families do not realize is that the decision to play on a sports team (or other interscholastic team) is not as much a school or district decision as it is a league decision. Every team that plays in a league has guidelines that it must adhere to, otherwise it can't play in the league. Some guidelines include eligibility for four years (so if there is a 5th year senior, he generally cannot play), certain GPA [grade point average], etc. Athletic leagues keep these rules so that the competitions stay fair, and for the safety of all students involved.

Homeschooling families should also remember that if they were allowed to play on a public school team, they must meet eligibility requirements, which would likely include additional testing or others means to determine grade level work . . . where it otherwise would not be required.

Homeschoolers Should Be Denied Access to Public School Resources

Sherry F. Colb

Sherry F. Colb is a professor at Rutgers Law School in Newark, New Jersey, and a columnist for the FindLaw legal website.

A growing number of parents in the United States are home-schooling their children, as an alternative to sending them to public or private schools. For a variety of reasons, these parents believe that they can provide an equal or superior educational experience at home.

Yet even parents who home-school their children (whom I will call "home-schoolers") have begun to recognize the benefits of group after-school activities. And increasingly, they have become interested in taking advantage of extracurricular activities offered to children enrolled at public schools.

States, and individual districts within states, are split on the question of whether to admit home-schooled children into activities, such as sports teams, at schools that they do not attend. Some places give home-schooled children this option, while others do not.

The debate on the subject of access raises important questions about the meaning of a public school education, for those who opt in as well as for those who do not.

State and Local Taxes as Public School "Tuition"

One argument that home-schoolers make in favor of access to extracurricular offerings is simple: They, too, pay the taxes that finance the public school enterprise. Therefore, they claim,

Sherry F. Colb, "Should Parents Who Home-School Their Children Have Access to Public School Extracurricular Programs," *findlaw.com*, January 30, 2005. Reproduced by permission.

they are entitled to take advantage of the school's offerings to the extent that they and their children are interested in doing so.

Paying taxes is not the equivalent of paying tuition for public school.

They say, further, that their decision to educate their children at home saves public schools money. Paying to support the public schools, they explain, provides a free benefit to the enrolled students—funds for education without the expense of having to teach an additional student.

To admit the home-schooler's child into extracurricular activities is, on this reasoning, to provide one small part of the complete benefit package to which such outside students are really entitled, based on the "tuition" payments their parents make by paying state and local taxes.

This argument may sound persuasive, but it is based on a faulty premise about a taxpayer's entitlements. Paying taxes is *not* the equivalent of paying tuition for public school. If it were, then people who have no children, or whose children are grown, would not have any obligation or reason to pay. Yet we *all* pay taxes, regardless of whether we have children and of how many we have.

A Flawed Analogy

The reason that governments (and thus taxpayers) fund public schools is that every person living in our society benefits from an educated and well-socialized next generation. The people currently in public school are part of the general population that will be voting and running this country down the road.

Thus, though the children themselves undoubtedly benefit from going to school, the role of public school in the community's life goes well beyond the provision of benefits to individual students and their families.

By analogy, consider the government funding that goes to pay police officers' salaries. Such money subsidizes a service that we all wish to enjoy—the reduction of crime and the protection of our communities from destructive and violent behavior. As taxpayers, then, we can legitimately complain when police are not well trained, just as we can all complain when children are not properly educated.

But neither children who attend private (or home) schools nor private people who hire armed security guards are entitled to negotiate alternative packages for their own education or protection from the government. There is no direct correspondence, in other words, between payment and services, when it comes to taxes.

Public School as a Consumer Package

That being said, however, public schools *do* provide a benefit to school-age children and the parents who send them there: They educate those children and thus prepare them for careers, without charging a fee.

There is a flawed underlying assumption at work: that public school is an assortment of products that families and their children consume.

Home-schoolers who wish to enroll their offspring in extracurricular activities accordingly argue that even if they do not have *special* rights as taxpayers, they do have the more *general* right to send their children to public school, like everyone else in the community. This claim is a fair one.

If so, home-schoolers ask, why can't they send their children to some *limited* component of public school and not the entire program? As the home-schoolers suggest, the family that consumes only one portion of what the school has to offer, instead of the complete package, does seem to save the public schools money. It may thus seem unfair to permit only all-or-nothing consumption of the public school's benefits.

To provide an analogy, public libraries provide borrowing privileges to all members (and membership is free). Theoretically, then, one person could borrow a large number of books from the library. But that does not preclude another person's borrowing a very small number of books.

Benefits and Burdens

Doesn't the greater right to attend public school include the lesser right to participate only in extracurricular activities—as home-schoolers contend?

No. Once again, there is a flawed underlying assumption at work: that public school is assortment of products that families and their children consume, like a meal offered at a shelter. On this assumption, some children can consume the meal in part, rather than in whole. One should not have to eat broccoli in order to eat corn.

It is the reciprocity component of public school education that gets lost when families opt in for only some of what is offered.

This picture of education as a consumption item, however, is a bit like the picture of taxes as tuition. The opportunity to go to public school carries with it both benefits and burdens—and the burdens shouldered may ultimately yield general benefits to the larger society.

The benefits can include access to teachers, lessons, and classrooms. The burdens might encompass the responsibility to attend, to study the mandatory subjects, to complete the assignments, to demonstrate respect for teachers and for other students, and, more generally, to become a productive and valuable member of the school community. It is these burdens that become difficult to fulfill when a child does not attend school.

Partial Home-Schooling as an Option

A school might legitimately argue that a family should not be able to pick and choose benefits and burdens. Say that Sally Student is interested in mathematics and science, but not in reading or writing. She should not be allowed to exempt herself from the classes in which she has no interest. This is true, moreover, even if her parents agree to teach her reading and writing at home, so that she can achieve the same level of proficiency as the other children. Her presence in the various classes, in other words, is not just a privilege but an obligation as well.

Though home-schooling is permissible, then, *partial* home-schooling need not be. A school can rightly view as disruptive the menu approach to public school. One of the lessons that children learn at school is that each person has obligations to the group that do not depend on her own personal desires (or those of her parents). To be able to opt in or opt out would undermine the seriousness of the overall endeavor.

All of the mandatory curricular offerings are accordingly both *available to* and *required of* the attending students. It is the reciprocity component of public school education that gets lost when families opt in for only some of what is offered.

Extracurriculars as a Distinct Endeavor

Home-schoolers have a response to this argument, though. They protest that extracurricular activities are really not an inseparable part of public school education, in the way that reading classes are. After-school programs are simply an opportunity that children have for developing athletic and other skills.

On this view, there is coherence to the inclusion of home-schoolers in athletics and other extracurricular activities. A child can legitimately participate in one of two *independent* programs without participating in the other.

This argument may be the strongest home-schoolers can offer, but it, too, is not entirely convincing.

The argument at first seems plausible because extracurriculars are in fact categorically distinct from other subjects in the curriculum (hence the prefix "extra" in their name). They are not mandatory, and the students therefore gravitate toward the activities that interest them the most. Some students do not participate in any of them (and thus select the reverse of what home-schoolers want). The activities are primarily recreational, and grades are not ordinarily assigned.

A school can, for example, place conditions—both positive and negative—on participation in extracurricular activities.

The Eligibility Link

If Paul Pupil receives his schooling at home but shows up at P.S. 1 for basketball practice, home-schoolers can argue, he does not therefore generate the message that he lacks respect for the school. Such activities are logically severable from the "schoolday" curriculum.

The home-schooled student . . . is not part of the community in which her academics . . . and . . . interactive conduct will be in evidence to the authorities that run the school.

The U.S. Supreme Court has implied its concurrence with this view in *Board of Education of Pottawatomie v. Earls* a decision upholding against a Fourth Amendment challenge the drug-testing of all students who participate in extracurricular activities, precisely because such activities are optional and stand outside of the regular curriculum.

The separation, however, is not quite as clear as it might seem. A school can, for example, place conditions—both positive and negative—on participation in extracurricular activities. A student might have to maintain a minimum grade point average to join an athletic team, for example. Or she might need to avoid getting into trouble during the day in order to be eligible for particular (or all) after-school activities.

In either case, the school has drawn a direct link between one's performance, behavior and attitude regarding the regular curriculum, on the one hand, and one's eligibility for extracurriculars, on the other.

The home-schooled student, however, is not well positioned to be judged along these dimensions, because she is not part of the community in which her academics, classroom contributions, and other interactive conduct will be in evidence to the authorities that run the school.

A Message of Disrespect for the Public School

To understand further how home-schooled children who participate in extracurricular activities might detract from the atmosphere of a school, consider the reasons people keep their children out of public schools in the first place.

One major motivation seems to be the perception (or even the reality) that the public school in one's area does not have high quality teachers and/or students. Another may be the view that the values embraced by the school (and/or by families that enroll their children there) are misguided (or even evil).

If these beliefs motivate home-schooling, then the presence of home-schooled children after school—and their "in your face" commitment to avoiding the faculty and students during the day—can seriously undermine the morale of the children who attend public school. Sending one's children to extracurricular activities alone is a way of saying, "we don't think your school or you have much to offer us, in terms of intelligence or morality, but we like your basketball team, so here we are."

It is not obvious that teachers and students should have to contend with this disrespectful message, implicit in such after-school limited joining. Disrespect uncoupled from any real investment in the place can make life depressing for those on the inside.

The Option to Participate

As I noted above, though, there are states and districts in which home-schooled children do have the option of participating in extracurricular activities at public schools. In such places, public schools may choose to create a clearer separation between in-school and after-school activities. They may also limit the curricular or behavioral conditions attached to joining extracurriculars and thus create a laissez-faire extracurricular world.

In such a world, participants must observe the rules of the game, compete for competitive positions, and otherwise conduct themselves in the way they might do in a publicly funded program that has nothing to do with the public school system.

This is perhaps the vision that home-schoolers have of extracurriculars everywhere. For schools that take a different and more holistic approach to education, though, this may represent an unwelcome state of affairs. And it is one that neither taxpayers nor a reciprocity-based public educational system should have to embrace.

Sports Are an Extension of the Classroom and Should Thus Exclude Homeschoolers

Preston Williams

Preston Williams writes a weekly column about high school sports in the Washington, D.C., area for The Washington Post.

As Aesop's fables for the cynical age, "Seinfeld" can provide insight into just about any life situation, even the ongoing debate about whether home-schooled students should be allowed to play on public high school sports teams.

There's an episode in which a floundering George Costanza is trying to figure out what career to pursue after quitting his real estate job. He hits upon sports broadcaster.

"Well," skeptical pal Jerry says, "they tend to give those jobs to ex-ballplayers and people that are, you know, in broadcasting."

"Well, that's really not fair," George replies.

The joke is, of course it's fair. Just as it's fair for state high school athletic associations to prohibit home-schooled students from competing on public high school teams because they're not, you know, public high school students.

Parents who choose to home-school do so for a variety of reasons: because their child is ahead or behind academically, religious beliefs, family considerations or dissatisfaction with local schools. Whatever the reason, they have chosen to bypass the extracurricular activities that the local public school offers, including sports.

Public high school uniforms don't have the names of neighborhoods or school districts on them. They have the names of schools. Being an area resident doesn't make you a representative of the school. Going to that school makes you a representative.

If you're ineligible to walk across the stage in your cap and gown, then you should be ineligible to walk on the field with your cap and glove.

Turns out, though, that more of the country is taking a Costanza view when it comes to home-schoolers suiting up for sports. According to the . . . Home School Legal Defense Association, 15 states allow home-schoolers to compete on public high school teams, with a steady trickle of states opening their programs in recent years, said Chris Klicka, senior counsel for the organization. Some other states allow local school divisions to set policies.

Maryland, the District [of Columbia] and Virginia have resisted accepting home-schooled students on their teams, but a bill came up in the Virginia General Assembly that would have forced the Virginia High School League [VHSL] to allow home-schoolers to participate in sports at public high schools. The bill died in the House Education Committee.

The VHSL was concerned enough in the preceding days, however, to distribute an e-mail with information on how to contact state representatives. After House Bill 375 failed to gain traction, the VHSL sent out another e-mail saying, "We appreciate the efforts of all who contacted their personal delegate and senator to express their opinions and support of VHSL athletics and activities."

You can't stiff-arm the public school's curriculum, administration and teachers and then expect to roll into the parking lot at 3:15 every day for practice.

So, the issue is on the minds of the public high school brass, and some area counties allow home-schoolers to take up to two classes or join school clubs. Sports could be next.

The cause has a high-profile public face: University of Florida quarterback Tim Tebow, the 2007 Heisman Trophy winner and the first sophomore to win the award. Tebow was home-schooled in Florida but played for his local public school team, Nease High in Ponte Vedra, where he was a Parade all-American. Miami Dolphins defensive end Jason Taylor also was home-schooled when he played for a public school team in Pennsylvania.

The Tim Tebow Act, similar to the failed measure in Virginia, was proposed in Alabama [in 2007]. It, too, failed to make it out of committee, but it was to be reintroduced at the legislative session that began [in early 2008].

High school sports are supposed to be an extension of the classroom. You can't stiff-arm the public school's curriculum, administration and teachers and then expect to roll into the parking lot at 3:15 every day for practice like you're going to Gold's Gym for a workout. That's playing time or a roster spot that belongs to a regular student.

If public school parents are discouraged from transferring their children for athletic reasons, then students who aren't even in the school system shouldn't show up just for athletics. For many sports, the home-schooled student has other options, including home-school teams or leagues, rec leagues and church leagues. Some private schools allow home-schoolers to play.

Public high school athletes have to meet standards in regard to attendance, grades and behavior. If your punishment is being sent to your room and not to the principal's office, then a coach or school cannot monitor whether a player should be eligible. And, as Alabama school officials pointed out, a rogue coach could cajole his academically challenged star player into being home-schooled just to preserve his eligibility.

The main argument cited by those in favor of allowing home-schoolers to compete for public school teams is that the home-school parents are taxpayers, too. Continuing in that vein, the parents might be saving the school division money by not sending their kids to public schools.

Fine. But there are plenty of residents without kids. They're paying taxes, too, but they can't expect to walk in off the street and have access to the school facilities. Residents pay taxes for parks, libraries, roads and hospitals that they might never use, but their community is better off for having those services.

The Home School Legal Defense Association does not take a stand on the issue of home-schoolers playing in public schools, Klicka said, because there's no consensus in the home-school community.

Granting home-schoolers greater access to public schools would result in more governmental meddling into home schools, which most home-schooling parents do not want.

If we think long enough, we probably could come up with a "Seinfeld" analogy for that, too.

Organizations to Contact

The editors have compiled the following list of organizations concerned with the issues debated in this book. The descriptions are derived from materials provided by the organizations. All have publications or information available for interested readers. The list was compiled on the date of publication of the present volume; the information provided here may change. Readers need to remember that many organizations take several weeks or longer to respond to inquiries.

American Association of School Administrators (AASA)
801 N. Quincy St., Suite 700, Arlington, VA   22203-1730
(703) 528-0700 • fax: (703) 841-1543
Web site: www.aasa.org

AASA is the professional organization for more than thirteen thousand educational leaders across the United States. Its mission is to support and develop effective school system leaders dedicated to the highest quality public education for all children. AASA members advance the goals of public education, champion children's causes in their districts and nationwide, help shape policy and oversee its implementation, and represent school districts to the public at large. The organization's publications include *School Administrator* magazine, as well as numerous journals, e-newsletters, books, and toolkits.

American Homeschool Association (AHA)
PO Box 3142, Palmer, AK   99645
(800) 236-3278
e-mail: aha@americanhomeschoolassociation.org
Web site: www.americanhomeschoolassociation.org

AHA is a service organization created to network homeschoolers on a national level. It is sponsored in part by the publishers of *Home Education Magazine.* Current AHA services include an online news and discussion list that provides news, information, and resources for homeschooling families.

Education Law Association (ELA)

University of Dayton, Dayton, OH   45469
(937) 229-3589 • fax (937) 229-3845
e-mail: ela@educationlaw.org
Web site: www.educationlaw.org

ELA is a nonprofit, nonadvocacy organization open to anyone interested in education law. The association, which is affiliated with the University of Dayton's School of Education and Allied Professions, has been providing unbiased information about current legal issues affecting education in schools, colleges, and universities since it was founded in 1954.

Home School Legal Defense Association (HSLDA)

PO Box 3000, Purcellville, VA   20134-9000
(540) 338-5600 • fax: (540) 338-2733
e-mail: info@hslda.org
Web site: www.hslda.org

HSLDA is a national membership Christian organization of families who homeschool their children. Its goal is to defend and advance the constitutional right of all parents to direct the education of their children and to protect family freedoms. The organization supports homeschooling families by negotiating with local officials, serving as an advocate in court proceedings, monitoring federal legislation, and fighting any proposed laws perceived as harmful to homeschooling.

National African-American Homeschooling Alliance (NAAHA)

e-mail: info@naaha.com
Web site: www.naaha.com

NAAHA is a nonsectarian organization and national online resource dedicated to providing timely and reliable resources for African American homeschoolers and anyone homeschooling African American children. Formed in 2003 to unite African American homeschoolers nationally, it is the largest homeschooling organization for blacks in America.

National Black Home Educators (NBHE)

13434 Plank Rd., PMB 110, Baker, LA   70714

e-mail: contact@nbhe.net

Web site: www.nbhe.net

NBHE is an online resource network founded in 2000 to encourage, support, and offer fellowship to families exploring the benefits of home education. The organization provides information about getting started in homeschooling, connects experienced families with new families, and recommends resources such as books, music, films, conferences, and curriculum.

National Center for Education Statistics (NCES)

1990 K St. NW, Washington, DC   20006

(202) 502-7300 • fax: (202) 502-7466

Web site: www.nces.ed.gov

NCES is part of the U.S. Department of Education and the Institute of Education Sciences and serves as the primary federal entity for collecting and analyzing data related to education in the United States and elsewhere. The center organizes training seminars, holds conferences, and publishes its findings in reports and publications, including the *Education Statistics Quarterly* and the *Digest of Education Statistics*.

National Education Association

1201 Sixteenth St. NW, Washington, DC   20036-3290

(202) 833-4000 • fax: (202) 822-7974

Web site: www.nea.org

NEA is a volunteer-based organization whose goal is to advance the cause of public education. The association lobbies legislators for school resources, campaigns for higher standards for the teaching profession, and files legal actions to protect academic freedom. At the local level, the association conducts professional workshops and negotiates contracts for school district employees.

National Home Education Network (NHEN)

PO Box 1652, Hobe Sound, FL   33475-1652
fax: (413) 581-1463
e-mail: info@nhen.org
Web site: www.nhen.org

NHEN is a volunteer organization that encourages and facilitates the grassroots work of state and local homeschooling organizations and individuals by providing information, fostering networking, and promoting public relations on a national level.

National Home Education Research Institute (NHERI)

PO Box 13939, Salem, OR   97309
(503) 364-1490 • fax: (503) 364-2827
e-mail: mail@nheri.org
Web site: www.nheri.org

NHERI is a nonprofit research organization that collects, tracks, and analyzes research on home-based education. A clearinghouse of research for the public, researchers, homeschoolers, the media, and policy makers, the organization strives to educate the public about homeschool research through speaking engagements, research reports, books, videos, and the journal *Home School Researcher*.

National School Boards Association (NSBA)

1680 Duke St., Alexandria, VA   22314
(703) 838-6722 • fax: (703) 683-7590
e-mail: info@nsba.org
Web site: www.nsba.org

NSBA serves the national and federal needs of local school boards. The association seeks to raise awareness of school board issues, assists school boards and educators in the uses of technology, reports the results of research on education issues, and lobbies Congress. NSBA publishes a variety of books and reports on school governance and other education topics, plus the magazine *American School Board Journal* and the newspaper *School Board News*.

United States Department of Education

400 Maryland Ave. SW, Washington, DC   20202-0498
800-872-5327
e-mail: customerservice@inet.ed.gov
Web site: www.ed.gov

The United States Department of Education works to ensure equal access to education and to foster educational excellence. The department establishes policies on federal financial aid for education and provides grants to primary, secondary, and postsecondary education institutes; financial aid to students for postsecondary education; and underwrites education research. It produces hundreds of publications annually, including *Community Update*, which informs readers about available resources, services, and publications.

Bibliography

Books

David H. Albert   *Have Fun. Learn Stuff. Grow. Home-schooling and the Curriculum of Love.* Monroe, ME: Common Courage, 2006.

Mimi Davis   *So—Why Do You Homeschool?* Longwood, FL: Xulon, 2005.

David d'Escoto and Kim d'Escoto   *The Little Book of BIG Reasons to Homeschool.* Nashville: B&H, 2007.

Milton Gaither   *Homeschool: An American History.* New York: Palgrave Macmillan, 2008.

Rachel Gathercole   *The Well-Adjusted Child: The Social Benefits of Homeschooling.* Denver: Mapletree, 2007.

Christopher J. Klicka   *Home School Heroes: The Struggle and Triumph of Home Schooling.* Nashville: B&H, 2006.

Martine Millman and Gregory Millman   *Homeschooling: A Family's Journey.* New York: Penguin, 2008.

Tamra B. Orr   *Asking Questions, Finding Answers: A Parent's Journey Through Homeschooling.* Tonasket, WA: HEM, 2008.

Brian D. Ray   *Worldwide Guide to Homeschooling: Facts and Stats on the Benefits of Homeschool.* New York: Palgrave Macmillan, 2008.

Lisa Rivero   *The Homeschooling Option: How to Decide When It's Right for Your Family.* New York: Palgrave Macmillan, 2008.

Bonnie Kerrigan Snyder and Mark Robert Snyder   *Public School Parent's Guide to Success: How to Beat Private School and Homeschooling.* Lincoln, NE: iUniverse, 2007.

Jack F. Troy   *School's Out: The Case for Abandoning Failing Public Schools and the Rebirth of American Education at Home.* Lincoln, NE: iUniverse, 2007.

Amy Schechter Vahid and Frank Vahid   *Homeschooling: A Path Rediscovered for Socialization, Education, and Family.* Lulu.com, 2007.

Gary Wyatt   *Family Ties: Relationships, Socialization, and Homeschooling.* Lanham, MD: University Press of America, 2008.

Periodicals

Michelle Conlin   "Meet My Teachers: Mom and Dad," *Business Week*, February 20, 2006.

Bruce S. Cooper and John Sureau   "The Politics of Homeschooling— New Developments, New Challenges," *Educational Policy*, January–March 2007.

Christa L. Green and Kathleen V. Hoover-Dempsey — "Why Do Parents Homeschool?" *Education & Urban Society*, February 2007.

Chloé A. Hilliard — "The New Home Room," *Village Voice*, April 9, 2008.

William G. Howell, Martin R. West, and Paul E. Peterson — "What Americans Think About Their Schools," *Education Next*, Fall 2007.

Eric J. Isenberg — "What Have We Learned About Homeschooling?" *Peabody Journal of Education*, Issue 2/3, 2007.

Christina Sim Keddie — "Homeschoolers and Public School Facilities: Proposals for Providing Fairer Access," *NYU Journal of Legislation and Public Policy*, Spring 2007.

Virginia Kelley — "Home Schooling: Beneficial, or Not?" University of Mississippi *Daily Mississippian*, May 29, 2008.

Dan Lips and Evan Feinberg — "Homeschooling: A Growing Option in American Education," *Heritage Foundation Backgrounder*, April 3, 2008.

Sandra Tsing Loh — "Tales Out of School," *Atlantic Monthly*, March 2008.

Neil MacFarquhar — "Resolute or Fearful, Many Muslims Turn to Home Schooling," *New York Times*, March 26, 2008.

Gregory J. Millman — "Home Is Where the School Is," *Washington Post*, March 23, 2008.

Brian D. Ray   "The Evidence Is So Positive: What
                      Current Research Tells Us About Ho-
                      meschooling," *Old Schoolhouse Maga-
                      zine*, Winter 2006–2007.

Michael H.   "Revisiting the Common Myths
Romanowski   About Homeschooling," *Clearing
                      House*, January/February 2006.

Robert Sanborn,   "Four Scenarios for the Future of
Adolfo Santos,   Education," *Futurist*, January/
Alexandra L.   February 2005.
Montgomery,
and James B.
Caruthers

Michael Smith   "Acceptance Grows but Myths Per-
                      sist," *Washington Times*, May 19,
                      2008.

Paula Wasley   "Home-Schooled Students Rise in
                      Supply and Demand," *Chronicle of
                      Higher Education*, October 12, 2007.

Kimberly A.   "Education Off the Grid: Constitu-
Yuracko   tional Constraints on Home School-
                      ing," *California Law Review*, February
                      2008.

Mary Ann Zehr   "U.S. Home Schoolers Push Move-
                      ment Around the World," *Education
                      Week*, January 4, 2006.

Index